What Is It Like to Be Alive?

ALSO BY CHRIS ARTHUR

Irish Nocturnes
(The Davies Group, 1999)

Irish Willow
(The Davies Group, 2002)

Irish Haiku
(The Davies Group, 2005)

Irish Elegies
(Palgrave Macmillan, 2009)

Words of the Grey Wind
(Blackstaff Press, 2009)

On the Shoreline of Knowledge
(University of Iowa Press, 2012)

Reading Life
(Negative Capability Press, 2017)

Hummingbirds Between the Pages
(Ohio State University Press, 2018)

Hidden Cargoes
(EastOver Press, 2022)

What Is It Like to Be Alive?

FOURTEEN ATTEMPTS AT AN ANSWER

CHRIS ARTHUR

Essays

ISBN: 978-1-958094-51-8

Anders Hilding's photo "A little boy with a horse in winter, 1958, Sweden" is held in Landskrona Museum's collection. Used by permission.

George Rodger's photo, "1945, Belsen, a Dutch Jewish boy walks through the camp." The *LIFE* Picture Collection © Used by permission.

The James McIntosh Patrick painting "The Tay Bridge from my Studio Window" is owned by Dundee Art Galleries and Museums. Used by permission.

EastOver Press encourages the use of our publications in educational settings. For questions about educational discounts, contact us online: www.EastOverPress.com or info@EastOverPress.com.

Book Design by Beste M. Doğan

10 9 8 7 6 5 4 3 2 1

Published in the United States of America by

EASTOVER PRESS
Rochester, Massachusetts
www.EastOverPress.com

For Jane,

who has

added so

much

to my

experience

of

being alive

Understand, I am always trying to figure out
what the soul is,
and where hidden,
and what shape—

MARY OLIVER

CONTENTS

INTRODUCTION

The essays in this book all address one question: What is it like to be alive? But my "fourteen attempts at an answer" explore such a diversity of subjects that, far from being thematically linked by a shared interest, they may appear more like unrelated pieces that don't belong together. A quick survey of the ground they cover certainly suggests that readers are being invited on a journey through some very varied territory:

- The plight of prostitutes in seventeenth-century Japan
- Watching ferrets in twenty-first-century Wales
- The fragments of memory captured in a school photograph
- Reading a photograph of a little boy with a horse, taken in Sweden in 1958

- Assessing how best to approach knowledge of the Holocaust
- Different ways of seeing the statue of a controversial Irish warrior
- Exploring aspects of a ninth-century Pictish burial site in Scotland
- Creativity and aging
- Learning to see goldcrests
- Becoming aware of time's scale through a patch of lichen
- Problems and possibilities in retrieving childhood memories
- The sense of existential absurdity maps can spark
- Describing the cargo carried by an ordinary moment
- Thoughts of mortality sparked by memorial plaques on park benches

Does this not suggest a chaotic swarm of footprints, each following its own path, rather than a neat line of tracks all headed in the same direction?

In one sense, yes, *What Is It Like to Be Alive?* is—quite deliberately—a varied collection. I hope it displays a healthy diversity of content. But for all their dissimilarity, the essays' points of entry soon lead into the same territory. If that territory had to be given a name—beyond simply saying it's where the question "What is it like to be alive?" is considered—perhaps Alexander Smith's "the infinite suggestiveness of common things" might be pressed into service as a description. Whatever we decide to call it, this is somewhere that's attuned to notes beyond the hum of the quotidian. Each of these fourteen essays starts from something ordinary. But what's easily dismissed as unremarkable soon reveals threads that lead to destinations that are quite astonishing. Exercises in seeing beyond the obvious, all of the essays look into life's mirror and offer their account of what they see there, shimmering elusively behind the obscuring immediacy of surface reflections.

* * *

The essay that provides my title was pivotal in supplying the cognitive coagulation that drew the book together. It helped me to see the bloodline of ideas snaking through the individual essays. This creates the relatedness that makes them a family. My guiding question brings sufficient focus to avoid accusations of assembling a miscellany of unrelated items, but it's not a strict enforcer of uniformity and order—such things are anathema to essay writing. Instead, the question acts as a lightly drawn emblem; it traces out a genetic watermark of belonging. In response to it, I've ranged over a spectrum of ideas. The value of asking "What is it like to be alive?" lies not so much in the specifics of any of the countless answers that could be given as in the space for reflection that it opens up—the way in which thinking about it attunes the mind to notes that can be missed if we only listen in the register set by our everyday preoccupations.

* * *

What Is It Like to Be Alive? is, unashamedly, an essay collection. That means it's not bound by the kind of linear progression that some books follow, plodding their way, step by predictable step, from introduction to conclusion. The modus operandi of the essay is less regimented, more mercurial. Each of my fourteen attempts at an answer is independently intelligible on its own terms rather than being a fraction of some wider calculation. Each essay is obedient not to any overarching plan but to the dynamics of its own unfolding. In putting them together as a collection I don't want to pretend they offer a unified narrative, or that one follows logically from another. Cumulatively, the essays reinforce and reiterate each other's concerns. And I like to think that read together they'll lay upon the reader's mind more forcefully than any on its own could manage the cadence of the voice behind them. Hearing that voice is close to the raison d'être of this genre—for "at heart," as Graham Good puts it, "the essay is the voice of the individual." I've arranged the constituent essays in a way that I think maximizes their reciprocity, but that doesn't mean the book needs to be read in this, or indeed in any, order.

* * *

The epigraph, from Mary Oliver's marvelous poem "Bone," is not meant to suggest that I'm on some sort of religious quest, or that I give credence to the simplistic sense of soul that sees it as a kind of homunculus inhabiting our flesh, an ethereal essence within our lumbering corporeality. I see it rather as convenient shorthand for precisely what is sought in explorations sparked by asking questions like "What is it like to be alive?" It's a term that indicates a realm beyond the commonplace where a sense of wonder at existence blazes, accompanied by amazement at our fleeting sentience. Without wishing to map the relationship between soul and language, I agree with Sven Birkerts that there's significant linkage between them. He puts it nicely when he says, "Language is the soul's ozone layer and we thin it at our peril." Whatever else it achieves, I hope *What Is It Like to Be Alive?* provides some robust and enriching thickening.

What Is It Like to Be Alive?

A Lament for Tama

On the wall beside her bed, Katie had stuck up a poster. Ignoring the landlord's stipulations forbidding Blu Tack, this was obviously what she'd used generously on each of the corners. There, telltale lumps were marked with the indentations of her thumbs, blunt craters witnessing to the pressure she'd applied to secure the bond. The poster was a pleasing Japanese woodblock print that was popular at that time. I'd seen it in several other student flats. It was a design that regularly appeared on mugs and T-shirts; there were postcard-sized reproductions of it too. Though I didn't know back then, it's one of Hiroshige's *One Hundred Famous Views of Edo.*

The perspective the artist has chosen puts the viewer indoors. We're in a room, looking out through a window at a view of fields and trees, with Mount Fuji in the distance. There's a flock of birds—perhaps geese—flying across the sky in the fading light of late af-

名所江戸百景
浅草田甫酉の町詣
廣重画

ternoon. The most striking thing about the picture is the white cat sitting on the windowsill. It's looking out at the same view as we are.

Beyond these obvious features, I'd no idea what the picture shows. I don't think Katie did either. She probably bought it because she was fond of cats, though her liking for Japanese art was also evidenced by a kimono-like silk dressing gown on the back of the door, decorated with swimming carp, and by a large poster of Hokusai's *Great Wave off Kanagawa*. This occupied pride of place above the mantelpiece and drew the eye as soon as you came into her room.

* * *

I'm interested in how easy it is to look at things and not really see what's there. Particularly when we get used to something, when it becomes a familiar part of the scene, we often don't notice the detail it contains. There's a great deal hidden in plain sight: our world is full of things that we see, but in such a cursory fashion that we miss a lot of what's there. If we stop to really look, examine closely what the glance takes in en passant, we often see something that's surprisingly different from what we had assumed was there.

If you added together all the time my eyes must have fallen on the Hiroshige poster as we lay in bed, I must have looked at it for hours. Even if I'd noticed the other things it contains, beyond the obvious elements of cat on the windowsill and Mount Fuji in the distance, I'd not have understood their significance. It was only years after those youthful days, long after Katie and I had gone our separate ways, that I came to understand what Hiroshige has depicted.

* * *

I think of the room's occupant as Tama. The cat is her haughty confidante, on whom she lavishes much affection. I wish she'd had a dog. It would have returned her feelings with more warmth than cats usually display. Then, whatever happened, she would at least have had canine loyalty and affection to rely on. And a dog would also have acted as a protector, keeping her safe from harm. But I realize that could have been problematic. Dogs can sense anger and aggression; they're adept at detecting threats, sniffing out danger. They recognize bullies. What if it had barked or growled at, or even bitten, one of the men who visited this room?

It's possible, but highly improbable, that the person who lived here really was called Tama. I take the name not from anything that Hiroshige reveals but from the composer of this haiku:

> Take me with you
> Fly free from servitude
> My kite

There are no kites in the view that Hiroshige gives us through the window, but there easily could have been; they're a common enough motif in his work. I imagine several fluttering in the sky on another day, sparking Tama's poem.

Who was she? Beyond her name as author of this haiku, very little is known about her. We don't know exactly when she was born and when she died, though she lived around the time that Hiroshige created the picture displayed in Katie's room. We can't even be sure if "Tama" was her real name. *In Zen Haiku* (2000), a selection of verses translated by Jonathan Clements and illustrated with Japanese prints from the Art Institute of Chicago's extensive collection, the note for her simply records that:

> Tama was a courtesan, kept imprisoned in a licensed red-light district. Here she asks to be set free. It is only in the final line that we discover she is talking to a paper kite that can neither hear nor help her—a fact that increases the sense of melancholy.

I picture Tama looking from the window that Hiroshige has drawn, seeing kites flying and envying their freedom.

* * *

The caption on the poster beside Katie's bed gave the title as *Asakusa Ricefields*. I can't remember if anything else was said beyond giving Hiroshige's name and the date of composition (1857). Perhaps it also noted something about the Torinomachi Festival, which accounts for the procession of people you can see if you look closely, making their way across the fields. But there was no information about the room or its occupant. In some sources that I've consulted since, nothing specific is said to support my making Tama the occupant of Hiroshige's room. For instance, in Douglas Mannering's popular *Great Works of Japanese Graphic Art* (1995) the emphasis is on the way in which the scene shows how "town and country were intermixed in Old Japan, making it easy to leave behind cramped and often squalid dwellings." We're told about the famous Buddhist shrine at Asakusa, dating from the seventh century, and how Hiroshige's view "brings together interior and exterior, cultivated fields and untamed nature, providing much to meditate upon." But Mannering tells us nothing about the room's purpose or the nature of the interactions between the people who used it.

Henry Smith's commentary, in *Hiroshige: One Hundred Famous Views of Edo* (2007), is more explicit:

> We are looking west from the second story of a Yoshiwara brothel over the area known as Asakusa Ricefields. We are in the room of a courtesan of middling rank.

The Yoshiwara was the licensed pleasure quarter of Edo, the city that became Tokyo. It's likely it was here that Tama was imprisoned. The Yoshiwara housed both common prostitutes and elite courtesans. Competition for ranking was fierce, but at whatever level it was enacted, the fundamental business was the same. Its nature is summed up in the roll of tissue paper just visible in Hiroshige's picture, lying on the floor below and to the left of the cat's tail. It's mostly hidden by a screen. This paper is known as *onkotogami*, "paper for the honorable act." Or to put it more bluntly, these are tissues for mopping up bodily fluids after sex.

* * *

Would Katie have had the poster on her wall if she'd known what it pictures? Perhaps. She really liked the white cat. Nor would she have been averse to having, as a kind of feminist icon, a visual statement of the sexual exploitation of women. But I suspect she'd have judged Hiroshige's take on this as too cosmeticized to allow it wall space in her room. She'd not have liked the way an ugly reality was prettified into an appealing image. And perhaps, like me, she'd have felt obscurely tricked when she discovered what the picture really shows—made to feel naive and gullible for not having grasped its import, guilty at having failed to see the injustice behind the aesthetic facade. I know she'd have sympathized with this unmet woman's unenviable situation and wanted to do something to change it, even though it was miles and years away and quite beyond the reach of any aid.

The prospect from Katie's flat was far less appealing than the one in Hiroshige's picture. The windows in her room overlooked a dingy cobbled street, on the other side of which towering buildings blocked off any view. The thrum and burr of city traffic created an almost constant background noise. At night it was quieter, but any silence was regularly broken by the blare of sirens and the loud clink of glass on glass as staff at a bar on the corner cleared the pavement tables. Defying the impossibilities of time, and their different cultural milieus and languages, I imagine Katie and Tama sitting together and talking. Despite the gulf between their life experiences, the freedom of one, the enslavement of the other; despite the different horizons of possibilities their lives offered; despite the different expectations their peer groups had of them—I'm confident they would have found common ground. I can imagine them laughing at male foibles, sharing their affection for cats, then turning serious as the shadow of violence, fear, oppression falls across their conversation.

* * *

Looking at the picture now, I'm struck by the part played in it by absence. The room's occupants can't be seen, but their presence is strongly hinted at by the things that are depicted. The cat is obviously cared for; it looks well fed and content. Beside the roll of *onkotogami* on the floor there's a set of decorative hairpins, miniature versions of the bamboo rakes known as *kumade* that were important accoutrements at the Torinomachi Festival. Decorated with symbols of wealth, they were sold in the stalls around the festival's main point of focus, the Washi Daimyojin shrine. This isn't shown in Hiroshige's picture (another absence) but is situated just to the right of the view he frames. The hairpins, sometimes referred to as "bear's claw" hairpins, mimic the rake shape of the full-size *kumade* that you can make out many of the tiny figures are carrying if you look closely at the procession that's crossing the fields. The symbolism isn't subtle: it turns on the idea of raking in prosperity. Two other objects are sitting on the windowsill to the right of the cat—a mouth-rinsing bowl and a towel beside it, lying in a way that suggests it's recently been used.

Henry Smith reads the picture this way:

> The courtesan has been visited by an afternoon customer. He brought as a gift the set of *kumade* hairpins, one of which has been pulled out and ad-

> mired. Now the tissue paper has served its function, and he has departed. The courtesan has washed her face and rinsed her mouth and is relaxing behind the screen to the left, opening the window to let in some cool air. The composure of the design reflects her relief and is implicitly set against the boisterous scene outside.

Or, since the roll of tissue paper looks as yet unused, another reading would be that a customer is still there and that "the honourable act" is being performed just out of sight, behind the screen. Perhaps the rumpled towel beside the bowl suggests a rapid rinse between customers rather than the relaxation Smith suggests. The cat's feline indifference gives no clue as to whether its pointed ears are hearing the sound of Tama's gentle, rhythmic breathing as she takes her ease, or the frenzied notes of sex.

* * *

Reviewing "Seduction: Japan's Floating World," an impressive exhibition at San Francisco's Asian Art Museum, Lisa Hix (writing in *Collectors' Weekly*) notes that "it's difficult to get a window into the world of Edo-period Japanese prostitutes without the gauzy romantic filter of the male gaze." The views we're given of this world by Hiroshige, Kunisada, Hokusai, Utamaro, and other artists are more like screens than windows, or—allowing for a degree of transparency—stained-glass lenses that decorate and distort rather than offer a literal record of what was there.

Looking at *Asakusa Ricefields* and thinking about the occupant of the pictured room, it's easy to slip into a kind of cherry-blossom caricature, an idealized version that takes the clean, bright lines and colors of the woodblock prints as its point of reference rather than the muddied realities beneath them. So I think of Tama as young and beautiful, a desirable woman of unlikely bodily perfection, clad in finery that yet hints at what lies beneath. She sits with self-assured poise and grace, awaiting a longed-for encounter with some Apollo-like figure of parallel perfection. They are of course in love. The honourable act will be performed with passion and tenderness. It will enhance both and sully neither. If I'm honest, I have a fleeting thought that sees me being there and doing it myself.

The shoddy coin of the transaction that bought her, her reluctance, the age and worry lines that mark her brow, her worries about the future, stains on her kimono, the smell of sweat, bruises left where her arms were gripped too hard, her memories of abuse suffered in childhood, the stretchmarks on her belly from an unwanted pregnancy, her dreams of freedom, the toothache that's been troubling her for days and taints her breath with the flavor of decay: all of this and more is censored out, caught on the other side of the romantic filter. All that gets through is the heady distillate of desire, a make-believe cartoon of compliant sexuality without commitment; pleasure shorn of responsibility or consequence; sensuality unbound and all allowed. Tama is reduced to a kind of pornographic cutout, her humanity—the individual she once was—the index of her dreams and fears, her daily preoccupations, her pleasures and pains, all unacknowledged. The art from that time, through whose tropes I see her, blinkers, even blindfolds, rather than constructing an accurate visual record.

* * *

Unsurprisingly, some early Western visitors to the Yoshiwara have left highly critical accounts. The title of a chapter in Clement Scott's *Pictures of the World* (1894), "Soiled Doves in Cages," catches the tenor of his outrage about how "the sanctity of women" was being abused. J. E. De Becker's *The Nightless City* (1899) condemns the Yoshiwara as "a very inferno of black despair" that is home to "concentrated debauchery and sexual perversion." Their Victorian morality was affronted by the spectacle they witnessed.

Our twenty-first-century sensibility is wary of the arrogance of criticizing other cultures. We're more accepting of different customs, more aware that our values are not universally shared. The bullish confidence of the nineteenth-century commentators, their sense of moral superiority to the "savages" they found in distant lands, now strikes us as naive if not grotesque. Cecilia Seigle's *Yoshiwara: The Glittering World of the Japanese Courtesan* (1993) is seen as the definitive work in English on this topic. It's written in a tone that would have puzzled Scott and De Becker. Throughout, she takes a nonjudgmental tone, explaining that her intention is not to condemn but rather to "transmit the views that prevailed and to acknowledge the cultural and social position the pleasure quarter then represented." My intention is different. I hope this will legitimate a critical note, without it edging into any sense of superiority or sanctimonious prudery. I don't want to write a phenomenology of prostitution as it was practiced at a particular time in a particular place. Rather, my intention is to think about one vanished individual and try to imagine how things might have been for her under the surface glamour of the woodblock prints. For Tama, what was it like to be alive? What was the flavor of her experience?

Clearly, what a contemporary Western view sees when it looks at the Yoshiwara is very different to how it would have appeared to the samurai culture that gave rise to it. That notwithstanding, to put it all beyond the reach of censure as someone else's valued cultural tradition, something we should respect and have no business criticizing, would seem a betrayal of principles rather than an expression of them. Yes, there are some positives. That the Yoshiwara inspired great artworks is undeniable. A licensed pleasure quarter may have been preferable to the chaotic situation that pertained before its regulation. A philosophy of carnal enjoyment is not without its merits. Life in the Yoshiwara may certainly have offered some individuals a better—or at least materially more comfortable—life than they could have expected had they remained in the impoverished communities they were born into. But do the child abuse and sexual exploitation that Tama and those like her were exposed to not belong in the same cluster of unacceptable behavior as female genital mutilation, so-called "honor killings," and other acts of violence toward women?

* * *

The title of the San Francisco exhibition mentions Japan's "floating world." What was meant by that? Perhaps the most famous definition is given by Asai Ryoi in his *Tales from the Floating World* (circa 1661):

> Living only for the moment, turning our full attention to the pleasures of the moon, sun, the cherry blossoms and the maple leaves, singing songs, drinking wine, and diverting ourselves just in floating, floating, caring not a whit for the pauperism staring us in the face, refusing to be disheartened, like a gourd floating along the river current: this is what we call the floating world, 'ukiyo.'

The art of this world, *ukiyo-e* (pictures of the floating world) focuses in particular on two subjects, the Yoshiwara pleasure quarter and the Kabuki theater district, two enclaves within Edo that are particularly associated with savoring pleasures and living in the moment.

It's certainly pleasurable to look at some of the magnificent woodblock prints created by the great artists for whom the Yoshiwara was an important subject. Hiroshige's *Evening Cherry at Nakanocho in the Yoshiwara,* for example, shows an engaging scene of courtesans, attendants, and customers walking under cherry trees by the light of a full moon. Like *Asakusa Ricefields,* it's an appealing image. Utamaro's *Lovers in an Upper Room* catches an intimate moment with understated delicacy, yet for all its restraint and discretion it manages to convey the potency of the encounter more effectively than many of the more explicit *shunga* prints.

There's no shortage of beautiful *ukiyo-e* work. But Laura Allen, who curated "Seduction: Japan's Floating World," warns us not to be seduced by the pictures. She urges us to "resist indulging in fantasies of Yoshiwara prostitutes presented in the artworks." Instead, we should try to imagine the real lives lived by the women portrayed—a task made difficult by the lack of firsthand accounts written by the women themselves.

In trying to resist fantasies, it's worth keeping in mind that *Yoshiwara* and *ukiyo* have both been manipulated so that the sense of the words has been changed into something different from the original meanings. *Yoshiwara*—the name of the area where the pleasure quarter was built—meant "Reed Moor." This simply referred to the marshy nature of the location. A slight shift in the written ideograms changed it into "Joyful Moor" or "Field of Good Fortune." *Ukiyo*, in its original Buddhist sense, pointed to the suffering that follows from desire. But "Suffering World" was magicked into "Floating World." I want to see past these verbal sleights of hand—and their visual equivalents in the beautiful work of the *ukiyo-e* artists.

* * *

Bring back to mind a line from Tama's haiku, her heartfelt wish to "fly free from servitude." What sort of servitude did she experience? Most of the women pictured so memorably by the *ukiyo-e* artists came to the Yoshiwara as children. Born into poor families, they were sold to brothels by parents who couldn't support them and for whom a girl child represented a valuable source of revenue.

Money would be given for a ten-year contract on a seven-year-old girl (or younger). The child could, at least in theory, gradually repay the amount paid for her—doing domestic chores, serving the older girls, and soon becoming a prostitute herself. But the reality was that debts incurred along the way—for food and drink and clothes—meant that the sum owed always increased and earnings didn't keep pace with it. Particularly if a girl was chosen to train as a courtesan, she needed an elaborate wardrobe and her own junior attendants. Everything came with a price. As Laura Allen notes:

> It was very difficult for them to buy out their contract because they were kept in debt the whole time. They were very rarely able to escape unless they were ransomed by a man who wanted to take them out of that world.

In the unlikely event that they did escape from the walled and moated confinement of the Yoshiwara, with guards posted at the gates, where could they go? Recapture was highly likely, and the result of that would be to lengthen the period of their incarceration. In *Geishas and the Floating World: Inside Tokyo's Yoshiwara Pleasure District* (1970), Stephen and Ethel Longstreet make clear the consequences for recaptured escapees:

> The cost of the hunt, the tips and bribes paid out to get her back were all added to her debts. Like a runaway convict who had years added to his term, so

a courtesan extended her slavery on being recovered.

It's likely Tama suffered the trauma of being sold into bondage in early childhood—whether by impoverished parents or as a result of kidnap, which was a common enough practice at that time. As the years of indentured labor passed, she'd have been groomed and trained, fitted into a niche in the hierarchical system that ranked women according to their potential to attract customers. At whatever level, she would have been readied for routine prostitution. In *Yoshiwara: The Glittering World of the Japanese Courtesan*, Cecilia Seigle points out that it was not uncommon for twelve- or thirteen-year-old girls to work as prostitutes. The brothel owners were hard taskmasters. Lisa Hix says that courtesans were "forced to work long hours even when they were sick or having their periods." They had to fulfill a daily quota of customers; to fail meant the imposition of a fine. Special holidays, known as *monbi*, added to their workload, with the quota increased. The Torinomachi Festival was one such *monbi*. If the courtesan failed to meet the target set for it, she had to pay the clients' fees herself. So Hiroshige's picture shows us Tama's room on one of the Yoshiwara's busiest days of the year, when the pressure to perform would have been intense.

Venereal disease, exhaustion, depression following terminated pregnancies, lead poisoning from makeup, alcoholism and drug addiction, anxiety, neuroses—such afflictions were common among the hundreds of women caught in the Yoshiwara's web of sexual slavery. Life expectancy was short. Hix records the stark fact that "many prostitutes died by the age of 20." And when they died, if there was no one to pay the funeral costs, as was frequently the case, they ended up in the Jōganji graveyard with little ceremony, where the remains of some twenty thousand prostitutes lie. These are the *muen*, the unconnected, cut off from the support of any family network.

This is the servitude from which Tama sought release.

* * *

How many "honorable acts" did you perform? With how many men? How many were gentle, how many rough? Was their attention ever wanted, or was each hand upon your breast, your thigh, each penetrating penis an affront? How much profit did others make from selling you? Was your body used so often, used so much, that you became numbed, resigned to sex as a daily chore, no more than the fulfilling of a contract in whose terms you were trapped? Were you ever adored? Reviled? Loved? Did any of your customers speak words of tenderness? Were there more compliments than curses? Was your sense of intimate trespass violated so much that something died in you, or did it kindle a cumulative rage? When clients were inside you, where were your thoughts? Dreaming of flying free as a kite, of being somewhere, someone else? Or were you focused on the particularities of the moment, the imperatives of sensation allowing no escape? Who tended you in illness, tried to ease your pain? And when you died (at what age?), was there anyone to tend your corpse? Was it handled respectfully, or just carelessly discarded, joining the thousands of other *muen* dumped in Jōganji's sad expanse? I have so many questions I'd like to ask. I wish there was some way for you to answer.

I'd be interested, too, to know if you ever felt minded, or pressured, into performing an act of *shinju*. *Shinju* can be defined as "the usually onerous, often self-maiming stratagems to which a prostitute might resort in order to convince a doubtful regular that she loved him and him alone, whatever her obligations as a seller of sex to others." I'm quoting from Lawrence Rogers's article in *Monumenta Nipponica* (1994), in which he looks at Fujimoto Kizan's *Shikido Okagami*. This is a written record by a Yoshiwara regular that details the different forms of *shinju*. These range from writing an oath, to haircutting, tattooing, tearing off a nail, or even amputating a finger. Such desperate measures might convince a patron that he was held in such special esteem that he "might even buy out her contract and free her from indiscriminate sexual servitude." That finger amputation was by no means an uncommon expedient in this desperate quest for some degree of freedom is shown by the fact that "the necessary paraphernalia"—the wooden pillows used as cutting blocks, the blades, the styptics and bandages to staunch the bleeding—were readily available for purchase. Lawrence Rogers recognizes that the unenviable reality of life for the prostitutes is easily lost sight of "as we peruse the gaily coloured woodblock prints." He suggests that reading Kizan's essay on *shinju* is a useful corrective to any romanticized picture, a reminder of "the grey obverse of the splendid prints."

This is the servitude from which Tama—and a multitude of others—sought to fly free. It is a sad fact of history that such dreamed of liberation rarely happened.

Of course I may have got it entirely wrong. In terms of gaining an accurate insight into the reality of Tama's life, it's possible that what I've said is as wildly off the mark as the version suggested by Hiroshige's picture. She may have found happiness. Perhaps she managed to escape, to find love, to enjoy comfort and riches. Maybe she lived life to the full and had few regrets, secured a position of power and influence, was blessed with long life, good health, a multitude of wanted children. I hope she did. But it seems unlikely. And even if, against the odds, some fairy-tale ending came about for her, for thousands it did not.

* * *

The Yoshiwara is gone now, finally abolished in 1959. But there are plenty of women ensnared in other varieties of sexual slavery around the world. How many—tens of thousands?—at this moment, as you read this sentence, will be looking out between the bars, literal or actual, of other windows, at other views, tissues strewn on the floor, a cat meowing somewhere, the heavy breathing of a customer sounding that unwelcome note they know so well? Trapped in some snare of poverty, human trafficking, drug dependency, fear, they'd no doubt share the sentiments behind Tama's haiku, yearning for their freedom.

In part, what I've written here is just a shard of memoir. I'd been looking through *Hiroshige: One Hundred Famous Views of Edo.* When I came to number 101 (for, despite the title, there are actually 118 views in this series) and saw *Asakusa Ricefields and the Torinomachi Festival,* I was immediately taken back to Katie's flat and the poster on the wall beside her bed. In part, it's an attempt to correct my earlier, naive seeing of this picture. But in the main what I want to set down is a lament for Tama. She's lent her name to the unknown occupant of this room, but I've also come to see her as representing not only the thousands of other women ensnared in the Yoshiwara's web, but those who are caught today in other versions of sexual exploitation. I suspect there's also an element of clumsy apology ghosting through my paragraphs. I know it isn't possible to make amends. I know what happened to Tama is not my fault. But I feel obligated nonetheless to say sorry. For what? For the objectifying male gaze, for those aspects of my gender that can cause such hurt. The drive to perform "the honorable act" can lead us far from anything remotely honorable.

I know that whatever I write, it won't make any difference. History has closed over what has happened here, the tonnage of the years sits upon it, entombing it forever in whatever shape it took. Tama's life won't be altered one whit by anything I say about it. But I still feel driven to say something for her, to leave a fragment of a record, a memorial of sorts, something that lets her voice shout out: "I was here!" "This is who I was!" "Here is the course my life took!" "Look at what happened!" "This is what they did!" "Remember me!" I'd like to think this essay has scrawled some sense of that on the walls of Hiroshige's tastefully appointed cell. Naturally, I don't know what happened within its confines—we're in the realms of empathetic imagination rather than documented fact—but I hope I have at least hinted at what may lie behind the picture and raised some questions that challenge the mute indifference of the white cat, the flying birds, and Mount Fuji in the distance.

Ferret Watching in Brynsteffan

Before introducing the ferret, whose rapid retraction provides the unlikely core around which these musings crystallized, let me give some coordinates of time and place to set the scene. "Brynsteffan" is my nom de guerre for a small town in rural Wales. The place and its denizens are real enough; you could visit them today. Given the correlation between the words on these pages and people's lives, the courtesy of some degree of protective obfuscation is demanded, an attempt to draw a literary equivalent of the net curtains that draped the windows of almost every house on the street I want to talk about. You won't find "Brynsteffan" marked on any map, nor will "St. Steffan's College"—the name I'm giving to its ancient seat of learning—be included in any directory of educational establishments. "North Street" can provide the camouflage for the real street where I lived for many years. Our semi-detached Victorian townhouse—I'll call it "Penbryn" in place of the name we actually gave it—stood halfway along the street, only a stone's throw from the college buildings. Every individual mentioned will be referred to only by a pseudonym. I hope this systematic anonymizing won't let the light of real identities glint through what I say. My intention is to comply with the code of authorial ethics that writers of creative nonfiction follow. Or, less admirably, by shrouding with these surgical drapes of pretense I'll feel readier to make the incisions that writing about people so often necessitates.

* * *

The ferret belonged to Jack, who lived next door. It was one of two he kept in a stilted cage under an apple tree in his back garden. Sometimes at night we could hear restless feral noises—a scrabbling at the wood and wire accompanied by high-pitched, growling chatter. Their rank scent drifted over the wall like a furtive memory from some half-remembered dream.

Jack was a tall, athletic-looking man in his thirties who rarely met your eye. He would walk up and down the concrete path that ran the length of his narrow garden, looking resolutely forward, ramrod straight. He never glanced from side to side. I wasn't sure whether this was because of shyness, or self-absorption, or a scrupulously territorial politeness that kept his gaze within the confines of his own property. Like a dog trained to keep to heel, he never allowed his attention to roam over the low boundary wall that separated our gardens. Once or twice, if I happened to be in our garden at the same time he was out in his, I tried a friendly greeting called across the wall. But this was met by no more than the faintest, most enigmatic of smiles. Such nonresponsiveness meant that I soon abandoned my attempts at across-the-wall neighborliness. Instead, we settled into a reciprocal pattern of silence and pretending that the other person wasn't there. So far as I could tell, Jack showed no trace of the awkwardness that, for me, always accompanied this pretense.

Jack's erect bearing, short hair, and conservative way of dressing gave away his army background. There was a military quality about his tweed jacket, ironed shirt, neatly pressed trousers, and immaculately polished brown leather shoes. He walked with parade ground deliberation. I'd heard he'd been a soldier once and guessed he bore the invisible scars of battle. But I never discovered what Jack's story was, so I can't be sure exactly how he was afflicted—only that some variety of affliction was de rigueur for anyone who lived next door. The house there had been divided into apartments and was owned by a local charity that was dedicated to providing temporary accommodation for the hurt and the fragile, those who'd somehow stumbled on life's way, whether on some inner demon or on one of the world's manifold cruelties and misfortunes. The previous person in Jack's apartment had been the most obviously troubled of the many tenants we'd seen come and go over the years. He left after the fourth fire in as many months, carried out on a stretcher to a waiting ambulance. His life seemed to consist of walking to the medical center to pick up his medication and spending the rest of the day, curtains closed, cocooned in the steady, repetitive thrum of loud, hypnotic music and whatever drugs he used to ease his pain. Whether the fires were accidental or deliberate we never knew, but for a while the blue lights and sirens of the emergency services were a regular occurrence on North Street. We weren't sorry to see him go.

Sometimes Jack walked his ferrets around the block, putting them in little leather harnesses attached to leads. The fact that they were semi-tame, well used to cars and people, meant that when one escaped from the stilted cage it didn't simply bolt; instead, it sought shelter under a car parked on the street just outside Jack's apartment. Alerted to its presence there by a passing neighbor who'd seen it dash for cover, Jack lay down on the pavement and gently reached his hand toward it, trying to coax it out. The ferret hesitated, then ran across the road with Jack in close pursuit. The little animal soon discovered a letterbox fixed low on one of the doors on the opposite side of the street. The terraced houses there have no front gardens; their doors open directly onto the sidewalk. Jack got there just as the ferret had nosed the letterbox open and was halfway in. He managed to grab the rear end of its body and swiftly pulled it back.

* * *

The house into whose hallway the ferret momentarily poked its head and forequarters before Jack whipped it out again, was occupied by a man referred to in our family simply as "Mr. Angry." What kind of life did he live there so close to us, his house just a few steps across the street from ours? We never knew for sure, but what we surmised was grim—though our picture was founded only on appearances, those treacherous clues to interiority that can be so revealing, and so misleading, about what goes on beneath them.

However much routine may blind us to it, there's a great deal of mystery sitting close at hand, right beside us, in the lives of those we see every day, but about whom we know almost nothing. In Brynsteffan, the unknownness of closely contiguous lives was accentuated by the rift that ran between the local Welsh-speaking community and non-Welsh-speaking incomers, like us, who'd been drawn to the place either by the low cost of housing or, as in our case, by employment at St. Steffan's College.

Since I'm Irish and my wife is Scottish, we were at least not seen as unwelcome intruders, as "The English" were—against whom there was considerable antipathy and, if truth be told, routine discrimination; an ugly, low-key racism. We were regarded as Celtic cousins, allies if not friends, the common bond between us formed by the belief that we'd also known the bitter taste of oppression by a powerful neighbor and so would be sympathetic to that old-established seam of local rancor (and it had indeed a flavor that we knew).

Despite being seen as Celtic cousins, we were still incomers, outsiders, non-Welsh speakers with no roots in the locality. As such, there was a considerable gulf separating us from the indigenous community. Whether our own shyness, reserve, or downright unfriendliness was responsible, or this Welsh-incomer divide, we never found out Mr. Angry's real name, so there's no need for me to invent a pseudonym; I can simply call him what we called him. Living on North Street for so long, we all became familiar with the aura of barely contained rage he carried with him, as if there was a just-suppressed fury roiling away only millimeters beneath the skin. The whole mien of the man—minatory, glowering, face set always in an aggressive scowl—suggested that his household enjoyed no great measure of domestic bliss. This impression was reinforced by the self-effacing manner of his timid wife and nervy teenage daughter. But we had no hard evidence for any kind of violence. Our imaginings may have been as off-target as whatever picture they had of us.

I'm not sure if Mr. Angry, or his wife, or daughter—or all of them—saw the ferret's head and forequarters appearing without warning in their hallway before Jack deftly engineered its rapid retraction through the letterbox. Had they done so, it would have been a disconcertingly surreal thing to witness. One moment there without warning, the next moment gone again with unnatural speed, it's the kind of near-hallucinatory occurrence that might make someone think they were dreaming, or imagining things, or going crazy.

* * *

What of it? Why give page space to so trivial an event? Is it worth thinking about the momentary appearance of half a ferret through some near stranger's letterbox in an insignificant town in rural Wales?

I'm not sure why, but imagining Mr. Angry or his wife or daughter—or all of them—seeing a ferret's head and forepaws suddenly materializing without warning in their hallway, only to have them instantly disappear, made me wonder about what else was happening along the street at precisely the moment this bizarre little cameo was flashing its occurrence across the few seconds that it occupied. Mostly, I paid little enough attention to that accustomed street, beyond the kind of automatic registering of things that provides the background to our waking moments, the rustle and hum of the familiar to which we give scant notice, the white noise of what we're used to. The unexpectedness of the ferret's momentary appearance in Mr. Angry's hallway snapped the fingers of attention; it woke me up to the passing of time in that place.

There was such a density of the unlikely distilled into this oddball circumstance that it seemed to leak a kind of luminescence beyond its own confines. It bestowed a glitter of estrangement on the familiar environs of North Street, making me look at them anew. The sheer speed with which the little creature was there and then gone no doubt also played a part, sensitizing me to the fleeting present, the fact that time is rushing by, and that each second of its passage, whatever cargo it carries, is sutured to a dwarfing tapestry of duration that contains eon-encompassing perspectives.

If you could isolate the few seconds in which the ferret appeared in Mr. Angry's hallway, freezing everyone in exactly the pose they happened to be in as the ferret poked its head through the letterbox, what would that moment on North Street look like? There's unlikely to be any of the crude drama we've grown used to from TV's endless loop of stories, their lurid narratives pacing things at an adrenaline-soaked tempo. This is far removed from the way in which life actually unfolds in a quiet place like Brynsteffan. Yet to me, for all their apparent dullness, the mundane scenes that would be dotted along North Street, the doings of my co-tenants of that ferret moment, are more interesting than any invented plotline, however thickened with the contrivance of shock and suspense.

Dusted with the speed and unlikeliness of the ferret's manifestation, that moment in North Street—whatever individual scenarios it contained—began to take on an almost numinous aura. I imagined fragments of multiple stories proliferating and interconnecting and tangling. If all the separate beads of experience could be considered simultaneously, the adjacent occurrences being played out in the fifty or so houses on the street linked together like a necklace, might we catch a glimpse of the shapes cut into history by the narrative torrent of our species?

* * *

From my study window I could see almost from one end of North Street to the other, so inviting the imagination to skip its way along from house to house, entranced by the provocative presence of this inviting line of prompts for possible stories, all laid out in a kind of serial suggestiveness. But Brynsteffan's setting was important, too. It's an isolated town, located amidst the fields and hedgerows of rural Wales. This means that far from being lost in some gigantic urban setting, where it might just have seemed one more anonymous street among many, North Street stands out as a thick thread of human habitation in a countryside that's sufficiently unpeopled to draw attention to the huddle of lives hosted in this cluster of houses.

Looking out the window I could see the precincts of the town quickly giving way to fields and hills and scattered woodland, interspersed with just a few farmhouses. As the only densely populated place for miles around, North Street caught the eye—yet it was on a scale that made it seem feasible to think from house to house, to wonder what each of its inhabitants might be doing at any given moment, without being defeated by the scale and anonymity that a larger town or city would impose. And the fact that I knew a scattering of people along the street gave the imagination a series of handholds; it provided points of reference that bestowed a steeling of credibility on any scenario I came up with.

I'm sure that if I could actually have observed the ferret moment as it unfolded in each of the houses along North Street, what I'd have seen would have been ordinary enough. A likely scenario might include:

> Mrs. Evans, newly widowed, sitting in straight-backed loneliness at the piano, playing a Chopin étude and thinking about her grandchildren in Australia; Dr. Davies, one of my colleagues at the college, grading student scripts, piled untidily on the table beside him, while his elderly mother dozes fitfully by the fire; the pretty girl from the bakery, who's just left school, enjoying her day off at home, watering the massive fern she keeps on a stand by her window and wondering if she's pregnant; Pete, a part-time lab technician at the local

> school—someone I know slightly from a writing group—reading *New Scientist* and drinking a cup of coffee; the Malaysian postgraduate student, who rents the house two doors down from us, fast asleep and in the midst of furiously contorted dreams, after another night of being repeatedly woken by her teething infant. The moment might find other North Street residents dusting, washing, excreting, gardening, watching TV, having sex, talking on the phone, arguing, writing . . .

In a way, it was as if the weirdness of the rapidly retracted ferret acted like a spark that fell on the tinder provided by my cast of mind, by North Street's location and straightness, and by the fact that over the years I'd had numerous glimpses of the lives lived there by my neighbors. The humdrum ordinariness of the place was quickly burned off as these combustibles caught light. In their flames, what was once familiar seemed noteworthy. Or to put this in a different way, Jack's rapidly retracted ferret acted to throw a kind of switch. It sent an awakening pulse of voltage surging through my outlook. Even thinking about it today, years later, long after I sold my house there and moved away, the jolt of electricity still makes me wonder about that moment, and about what's happening there right now, and how all the moments that have unfolded in Brynsteffan—and that will unfold there in the future—relate to each other and to the clamor of the world beyond it.

North Street's ribbon of humanness, its three hundred meters of moment-after-moment-after-moment existence, a tiny segment of our species' story, was like a kind of filament of exposed consciousness shining out its presence in the countryside. If the droplets of circumstance caught in this net of habitation were put together, what would they look like? And if to that catalogue of local particulars were added more and more adjacent occurrences, rippling out in ever wider rings to catch the ferret moment as it occurred *everywhere*, would any more meaning be evident in that massive pointillism of completeness than in the minute fragment of time underscored one afternoon in a small Welsh town when a ferret momentarily appeared through a letterbox?

* * *

Thinking about the possible tonnage of a moment as it quivers its way along the nerve of North Street, and about how it connects with the fabric of time on wider horizons—beyond Brynsteffan, beyond Wales—I found my musings moving vertically as well as horizontally. By this I mean that in trying to catch the flavor of the ferret moment I not only thought about what the present contained moment by moment, house by house, life by life all along the little segment of the world that North Street represented. I also wanted to grasp what the substrate was on which this flow of the present happened. On the one hand, the ferret made me think *along* the street, wondering about what was taking place in each house contiguously with the ferret's sudden appearance/disappearance. On the other hand, it made me think *down* so that I tried to mine the seam of space-time that was framed by the hallway of Mr. Angry's house.

What had happened there in that small area behind the door from the moment the house was built until the ferret's snout first touched the cold metal of the letterbox? What had happened there, in that exact same spot, long before there was a house or town or street here, long before the house was built, eons before there were such creatures as ferrets or humans roaming the world? And what will happen there long after all the denizens of North Street are as ancient as fossils now seem to us? Everything that happens here on this particular patch of earth adds another incremental layer of presence, contributes to the platform of history-in-this-place on which every subsequent moment performs its pirouette of individual specificity before it too becomes part of the ground that other moments walk on, laying its body down to add another sliver of temporal depth—the present repeatedly transmuting into the past.

From the title deeds of the house we bought on North Street—the property I'm calling "Penbryn"—I know that it was built in the mid-1800s and that we were the sixth family to have lived in it. The terraced houses on the other side of the street, Mr. Angry's among them, had been built about a decade earlier. Apart from one new house erected on a vacant plot sometime in the 1970s, all the houses on North Street were well over a hundred years old. So although they were by no means ancient, they didn't have the anonymity that many new-build dwellings possess. There were whispers of other lives in our house, glimpses of other moments. One elderly neighbor told me she'd been born in the room I used as my study; another said, almost apologetically, that her father had died in our bedroom; an electrician who came to rewire the property shortly after we moved in turned out to be a previous owner's son who, as a boy, had been frightened of the cellar. A teacher at the local primary school, just along the road, remembered playing in the garden as a child.

These snippets of Penbryn's oral history, coupled with the names and dates given on the title deeds, provided texture and momentum for my musings about the ferret moment. They gave depth to it, showing how whatever passed here now was underlain by numerous strata of other occurrences. And of course the reach of documentation and spoken comment is paltry compared to the scale of the massif of time on whose millions-of-years' depth Penbryn, like all the other houses on the street, was built. It is on that massif's surface that everyone skitters along, our thin wafer of moments, the crust of the present, formed over unfathomable depths.

* * *

I never set foot in Mr. Angry's house, but I did occasionally see inside the hallway. Sometimes, if he was ferrying things to or from his car when it was parked at the curbside, he left the front door of his house open. If I happened to be walking past, I couldn't resist peeping in. From these glimpses I had a vague impression of a loudly patterned floral carpet in yellows and oranges, and ornate wallpaper with some sort of dark design of swirling leaves. There was an oval mirror facing the street; its bright reflective surface always caught the eye. But the thing I noticed most from these occasional, furtive glances was an imposingly tall grandfather clock whose loud tick-tock was clearly audible to passersby. I know the dimensions of a moment are uncertain—who knows where one begins or ends—but for me it was this fleeting unit of measurement, the grandfather clock's loud tick-tock, that seemed to define the duration of the moment that so fascinated me: tick, the ferret appears; tock, it vanishes again. In fact, I came to imagine Mr. Angry's clock beating like a metronome, dicing time into those little snapshot moments of life in which the events that happened on North Street took place. The clock's drumbeat rhythm seemed like a pulse. It sounded out a tocsin that quivered through us, made us galley slaves of time: pull on the oars, tick, you're born; pull again, tock, you die; tick, and the next generation enters.

A moment in its totality is impossible to grasp. Even if we cut it down to a single tick-tock in one house in one street in one small town in Wales, it's hard to formulate a picture of the shape, extent, or texture of what happens, or determine what it tells us, or see the depths on which it surfs its momentary manifestation before it too adds its presence to the oceanic mass of history. We may glimpse some hint of the nature of time's passing if we focus on our immediate surroundings, try to see—if only for one ferret instant—what's happening around us. But joined inseparably to each tick-tock—embedded in the very DNA of every second—there is no less than the rest of time leaning its weight upon us. No wonder, then, that when we split the atom of the humdrum, the radiance released is so astounding.

In Transition

While primary schools in the UK now tend to have a straightforward numerical system, with pupils starting in P1 and going through to P7 before leaving for secondary, the school I attended described things differently, though the year-by-year advancement was the same. The first class we entered, when we started school at five years old, was known to everyone as “Ducks.” I’ve no idea why this name was chosen. It only seems odd to me now, looking back. At the time we didn’t think to question it; it was simply part of the established patois of the place. After a year in Ducks we went into the more prosaically named “Upper Kindergarten.” Then, as if to make amends for such a bland descriptor, the next class was called “Transition.” That was a word I’d not met before, and I’ve no memory of its ever being explained to me. I liked the exotic sound of it; it seemed to shimmer with a kind of silvery percussion that made me think of tambourines. What it meant outside of school was immaterial, for us it was simply the name that indicated a particular class that occupied a particular room and that was taught by a particular teacher. If it had been called "Hens" or "Ants" or "Tertiary," it would have made no difference to us. Almost any word would have sufficed to play the simple designatory role that in our ears was all that "Transition" did.

Why "Transition"? Again, the oddness of the name only strikes me now, decades later. When I was at school it didn't seem peculiar at all; it was simply the way things were, a given of the system, part of the tradition of the place and, as such, like "Ducks," accorded the uncritical acceptance of what we were used to. But I wonder now what kind of transition we were thought to be going through at that stage of our school careers. It would have made more sense if the first year had been given that name instead of "Ducks," marking the considerable transition that's involved in moving from the world of home into the world of school. Likewise, a case could be made for calling the last year at primary "Transition," since it saw us poised to make the move into the much larger setting of the secondary school.

But why call our third year in primary "Transition"? What were we thought to be transitioning between at that point in our lives? The move from Upper Kindergarten into Transition or from Transition into P1 involved no significant upheaval in terms of physical location or scale. All the classrooms were closely adjacent, in the same familiar building. There was no daunting influx of new pupils or new teachers and subjects, nor did we seem to be going through any dramatic developmental change; at that age we were still too young for the disruptive storms of adolescence to make their presence felt. Other thresholds seemed to warrant the title "Transition" far more than whatever one we were thought to be crossing between the ages of six and eight.

* * *

Transition, from the Latin *transitus, transitio,* meaning to go, is all about movement. It indicates no fixed position but rather an interim, passing state, part of a continuing process. The word can be defined as "a passage from one place, stage, style, or subject to another." Being in transition means that you're in transit; instead of standing still you're moving, or being transported, from one locus, phase, or mindset to another. Change is built into *transition*'s verbal DNA.

Whenever I hear the word now I'm reminded of a comment of Montaigne's in his essay "On Repentance":

> The world is but a perennial movement. All things in it are in constant motion—the earth, the rocks of the Caucasus, the pyramids of Egypt—both with the common motion and their own. Stability is nothing but more languid motion.

In other words, everything is in transition; movement is indelibly ingrained in the deep structure of all that we experience.

Montaigne's ideas about perennial movement have much in

common with the Buddhist concept of *anicca,* or impermanence. This is something that's threaded so completely into every aspect of being that it's considered by Buddhists to be one of the basic characteristics of existence. Not that I had any concept of *anicca* in Transition. At that age I didn't even know that Buddhism existed, let alone what its teachings were. *Anicca* was part of the cognitive cargo that would spark a change in thinking in the years ahead, part of my transition from a conservative Ulster Presbyterian upbringing to a point of view informed by ideas taken from a range of Eastern traditions. But that lay far ahead. When I was in Transition, my cognitive horizons were determined by the milieu in which I found myself, and it had no place for Buddhist ideas.

As a corollary to his recognition of constant motion—change as an integral and intimate part of the fabric of things—Montaigne goes on to note the key characteristic of his writing: "I do not portray being; I portray passing." And for Montaigne, *passing* didn't just mean "passing from one age to another," the kind of ordered steps that can be imagined as we progress from year to year, following a sequence that's sufficiently gradual we can foster the illusion of static points along the way. Rather, he had in mind something more intense, more all-pervasive: namely, the passing that occurs "from day to day, from minute to minute." It's been a long while since I graduated from my Transition class at school, but the sense that everything is passing, an awareness of being in and surrounded by transition, is something that's grown stronger in the years since then.

* * *

What made me think of my "Transition" class again, nearly half a century after leaving it? My attention was turned in this direction by receiving news of a classmate's passing through another transition, one that makes the move from primary to secondary school seem trivial. Barbara had crossed the threshold from life into death.

It's hard to take in the death of anyone you know, to accept the full, stark, nonnegotiable reality of the fact they've gone, that you'll never see them again, or hear news of any of their doings. Such total loss somehow goes against the grain of believability, which is odd given the inevitability of death and the centuries through which, as a species, we must have grown accustomed to its presence. Yet I suspect I'm not alone in often doubting the first news of someone's death. My immediate reaction is that there must be some mistake. My informant must have got it wrong. Somewhere along the way lines have been crossed and inaccurate information given. I don't like to offer condolences until I see a formal death notice. That, too, I'm initially reluctant to believe, but seeing it written down somehow bestows the imprimatur of certainty that word of mouth, for all I know I should believe it, can't quite summon on its own.

Although I'd been told that Barbara had been seriously ill, hearing that she'd died sparked this initial sense of disbelief. Even while knowing it was true, that no one would make it up or get it wrong, there was still a part of me that felt it couldn't be correct. Perhaps the doubt was stronger because I'd not seen her for so long. My image of her was still governed by the child she'd been in Transition. Despite

knowing that she'd grown up, had a successful career, got married, had children of her own—none of this is how I think of her. To me, her name still brings to mind the lively energy of the seven-year-old I remember from our schooldays. Perhaps if I'd known her in her sixties it would have eclipsed these early memories and made the idea of her dying seem less preposterous than it did.

On its own, hearing that Barbara had succumbed to cancer would only have caused one of those moments of mingled disbelief, sadness, and regret that grow commoner with age. Soon enough the news would have properly sunk in, bedding down in the mind with the weight of its unwelcome certainty, displacing from the nest of hope any lingering doubt about its truth, like a monstrous cuckoo chick ejecting the nestlings of its host. A jumble of childhood memories about her might have played through my thoughts for a while, but they'd have faded soon enough. The reason her death has had the depth of impact that it has, why it's made me stop, reflect, and write about it here, is that it sent me back to an old school photograph of our Transition class, a framed group portrait in black-and-white that I haven't looked at for years. Looking at it again in light of the news of Barbara's death has made me realize anew something I really know but not infrequently forget—namely, the extent to which I'm still in transition, along with everybody else.

Descriptions of photographs can easily become tedious, so I'll keep this one brief—particularly since what interests me is something that can't be seen. There are twenty-five of us in the picture, twenty-six if you count our teacher, the redoubtable Miss

Watt. We're grouped at the front of the school building, trying, with varying degrees of success, to keep still and hold a pose for the photographer. It's a struggle, given the restless energy of children of that age. We've been arranged in three rows. Those in the front one are seated on wooden benches taken from the dining hall. Miss Watt sits in the middle, center frame. Her chair is flanked on each side by a bench on which five children are sitting. Moving left to right they're arranged girl-boy-girl-boy-girl, then Miss Watt, then the same sequence again on her other side. Behind Miss Watt there's a standing row, again of ten pupils and again arranged in alternating genders, but this time boy-girl-boy-girl-boy. Miss Watt's head, level with those standing in this second row, is used as a kind of repeat marker so that the boy-girl-boy-girl-boy sequence is played out again on her left. The third row must be standing on a bench. It's not visible, but its presence can be inferred from the way the five pupils on it are elevated above everyone else. The five are also centered on Miss Watt, two girls, a boy, then two more girls.

Barbara is the second left of the five pupils standing in the back row. She's a pretty, dark-haired girl whose air of self-possession and confidence seems evident in her expression and how she holds herself. But of course I might be reading my memory of these qualities into the photograph rather than interpreting visual cues that are present for anyone to see. It's always hard to know how much we read out of the world and how much we read into it.

* * *

Although it must have been a notable event in the quiet routine that ruled our time at school, I don't remember anything about the day the photograph was taken. I imagine we were pressed into service to carry the wooden benches from the dining hall and to take them back again once things were completed. The setting chosen for the photograph was just outside the school's front door. The photographer must surely have spent time arranging us into the group that's pictured. It seems likely this would have occasioned squabbles since we're separated from friends. But no doubt his instructions would have been reinforced by Miss Watt's iron hand. For all her diminutive stature and benign smile for the camera, she was a formidable disciplinarian with a fiery temper. None of us took liberties with her.

The school building was an elegant Georgian-style house that had once been a family home. Behind us you can see the windows of the two downstairs classrooms, located on either side of the front door. These were occupied by P2 and P3. Ducks, Transition, and P1 were upstairs; P4 occupied a separate annex in the yard. The front door is shut, which it never was during school hours, no doubt to help give definition to the photo. If I had to guess, I'd say the door was painted blue, but whether that's memory or invention is at this stage hard to say.

We're grouped together on a gravel drive that—though you couldn't tell this from the photograph—swept down on both sides of a front lawn to the school's main gate, where mothers (never fathers in those days) clustered chatting, waiting for the bell that would signal the end of the school day and the release of their children back into their charge. The lawn was dominated by a large weeping ash tree whose branches brushed the ground. The ash tree would have been directly in our line of sight, behind where the photographer must have been standing. The spindly twigs of two small bushes growing on either side of the front door provide the only vegetation evident in the photograph. Judging by the just unfurling foliage, the photograph must have been taken in March. A shadow on the wall suggests a sunny day, but it doesn't look warm; everyone is wearing pullovers and cardigans. The school is in Lisburn, a town not far from Belfast. It's 1962, seven years before the onset of Northern Ireland's Troubles. If a photograph could record sectarian faultlines, they'd be visible all around us, already there, poised to fracture the country into the violence that followed.

* * *

I can pick myself out, of course, standing at the right end of the second row. I say "of course," but what I'm taking as obvious, a given, something that can just be automatically assumed is, I think, a far more recent thing than that casual "of course" admits. Did prephotographic generations carry with them into maturity a clear image of how they looked as children? Our ability to connect the way we are now with the way we were several decades previously is surely a skill that's been fostered by photography. Given the momentous changes that we go through from infancy to adulthood, the way in which appearance alters, the many differences our form presents to the eye at six months and at sixty, would we be able to identify the link between images of our present and past selves without an intervening catechism of photographs taken through the years? Their images provide the necessary stepping stones to create a visual chronicle of our aging; they allow us to pace ourselves with ourselves so that our previous iterations can maintain a connection with whatever shape our current form takes.

Whatever the exact mechanisms involved, I suspect that a lifetime of looking at photographs teaches us to see ourselves in ways not open to our ancestors. How much is our sense of self (and others) influenced by images? Do we really grasp what it is that photographs lay upon the psyche? What is it about the little boy in the photograph that lets me recognize him as me? If a stranger looking at me now were to be presented with the photo of my Transition class, could they work out which of the children I used to be? Are there sufficient similarities between us for such an identification to be confidently made, or do I make it because I'm following cues no stranger would have access to? I'm not sure how to answer this flotilla of questions, but rather than simply matching now and then because of obvious, self-evident likenesses that anyone could spot, I think I'm relying more on my memories of that class, my familiarity with other photos of myself from around that time—private knowledge that has let me learn the links in the chain of who I am, building up in mind a sense of what I looked like at different points in my ongoing transition through the years.

* * *

In his search for some enduring, unchanging essence that might be thought of as the self, David Hume concluded that no such thing exists. In the section on personal identity in *A Treatise of Human Nature,* he suggests—in terms reminiscent of Montaigne—that we are creatures of transition, characterized more by "perpetual flux and movement" than by anything fixed and static. The mind moves over a rapid succession of ideas, images, sensations. It is this that kindles our sense of consciousness, of who we are, rather than some separate nugget of identity that perdures through and is separate from this kaleidoscope of shifting states. Our visual identity is a similarly shifting, changing thing, however much single photographs may appear to catch us. Photographs are more a testament to change than to any constancy. Image succeeds image as we drift our way down the flow of time. Look carefully and no two are the same; change, *anicca,* flux, transition, motion—call it what you will—is written into all of them.

* * *

Looking along the rows of faces of my erstwhile classmates engenders a curious sensation. They act like a set of keys. Though some no longer fit any of my locks (there are a few faces I don't recognize at all), most slide smoothly into place, opening a selection of the honeycomb of cells that line the vault of memory. Out of them spill the few shards of recollection that were laid down all those years ago about the individuals concerned: the girl with ginger hair who was adopted; the boy who had spectacular nosebleeds; the girl who wet herself and the dusty wooden floor of the classroom, occasioning the fetching of a clattering bucket and mop; the boy who needed glasses to see what was written on the blackboard; the girl whose skin was like sandpaper because of eczema. Sometimes the fragments that have been retained are about parents and home life: the boy whose family owned a local pub, their association with liquor raising questions about their respectability; the girl whose father was rumored to have lost too many commercial properties to fire to make accident believable. At seven we'd not have grasped the nature of an insurance scam, but we were adept enough at reading the signs to know that our parents looked at him askance. One face prompts the memory "violent father who hit his sons"; another brings to mind a picture of the family's foul-smelling boxer dog; to another is spliced the memory of cutting my finger badly while playing at his house and having his mother dress it with cotton wool, much to the annoyance of my mother, who later had to pick numerous fibers out of the wound.

When I scan the faces in the photograph, this miscellany of memory shards comes prickling back. Familiar faces trip me up like hidden curbstones in the flow of time, the unevennesses they create made of these random fragments that are all I can remember about them now. No doubt, were any of them to look at the photograph and recognize me, any memories my face might trigger (and I'd be curious to know what these might be) would be just as fractional, as far removed from my sense of who I am, as my memories of them are to whatever sense of self animates their consciousness. Our images of others and of ourselves draw on such different aquifers of experience. My knowledge of my classmates was already partial, even before the eroding power of years is added in. For me, the fragments I recall about them are isolated slivers of lives observed. For those observed, they're part of an environing milieu experienced as an integrated whole. Everyone in the photo will have, or will have had, a sense of me-ness that's as strong as mine. In it the random standalone fragments I've remembered will have a completely different resonance. Far from being isolated shards, they'll be constituent parts of the complex web of personal experience seen from the inside, tightly woven into the chrysalis-continuum of self we all inhabit, that receptacle of changes that functions like a frame. Inside it are the people, places, and events, the thoughts and feelings that spin their influence on us, create our world, seem almost as close to us as our own blood and breath.

* * *

In her brilliant meditation *On Photography,* Susan Sontag notes the way in which photographs show people "irrefutably *there* and at a specific age in their lives." Photographs create patterns that "a moment later have already disbanded, changed," as people continue "along the course of their independent destinies." Where did we all go after that moment in 1962 when our Transition class was pictured in front of the school? What course did people's independent destinies follow? What stories do they tell? I know how my own future unfolded from that point in time, could plot it out in detail, mark in the usual milestones of significance: births and deaths and marriage, education and employment, travels, interests, aspirations and achievements, losses, fears, regrets. Around the single thread of my individual life story I could add something of the tapestry that creates the context in which it's set, the events of

1962, 1963, 1964, and so on right up to the present and my efforts to portray this vanished moment in these words. I could sketch at least some of what was happening at familial, local, national, and international levels as we sat for our Transition photograph, the fine detail of history that's woven around us moment by moment and the way in which every thread of our existence evidences a genealogy that runs back for eons. Everyone in the photograph could perform the same kind of exercise (those of us still living), drawing out their own presence and picturing the context in which it's set. Twenty-six life threads embedded in the tapestry of time, a tapestry whose warp and weft act like a kind of complex umbilical connecting us to a universe that's fifteen billion years old, to a galaxy that's just one of millions studding the amplitude of space.

Looking at the photograph I have a sense of fireworks paused, their incandescence frozen for a moment, dulled, preserved, their explosions of light and color stilled for just a heartbeat. What the photograph can't catch—but can nudge the imagination to picture—is the resumption of movement that followed, the twenty-six trajectories that stream out from this stationary image as, disbanded, we each embraced whatever unfoldings life held in store for us after the shared moment pictured on that long-vanished day at school.

* * *

In an idle moment I indulged in what's surely become a common distraction: I Googled names, curious to see if I could discover what shape the other lives had taken. With some I drew a blank.

With others I found identically named people whose prominence was such that their web footprint hid any trace of their more private namesakes. With one boy I used to know quite well, I found an obituary. He'd died two years before Barbara and I'd never heard till then.

The boy standing at the center of the back row, Harry, unexpectedly gave me an image that can be applied to everyone in the photograph. It stresses our transitional and transitory nature. On his website he includes a pictorial summary of his life. The central image, acting like a spine, is a river. It winds its way down the page, gradually widening with age. The idea of life as a river is hardly original, but it powerfully emphasizes its transitional nature, the way we're being swept along by time rather than standing still. Sometimes we may feel becalmed, the water around us may look unrippled and still, but whatever stage we're at is characterized by change and movement, not by any fixed state that endures. As Montaigne put it, apparent stability is nothing but "more languid motion."

On Harry's river, key dates are marked like vertebrae along its course, from his birth in 1954 to where he is today. Travels, interests, accomplishments are briefly noted, written in at the appropriate point in the river's flow. Who could have guessed that day as the camera shutter clicked on our Transition class that forty years later Harry would be attacked and left for dead in Nicaragua, where he was living at the time? As he lay recuperating from his injuries, did his thoughts ever stray back to Miss Watt and his year in her Transition class? Did he sometimes think of Barbara, who was standing next to him in the photo? Does he know she's dead? When he worked under armed guard in Iraq, doing educational work for the Mines Advisory Group, when he was with the UN, when he lived in America or Australia, did he ever wonder about what his old classmates were doing, where they were living, who had married whom? What was he thinking the moment the photograph was taken? What was he thinking yesterday? And what runs between these moments in the river of his life, weaving the necessary continuities that create his sense of being Harry?

* * *

What course did Barbara's life-river follow before the cessation of its flow? Did she sometimes look at the photograph of our Transition class, perhaps prompted to do so by receiving news of the death of another of our classmates? She's standing next to Harry, but I can't remember if they knew each other well, nor do I know if they stayed in contact as adults. Did their waters come close together, even intermingle, or diverge and follow completely different routes?

Though we were classmates for several years and our mothers were friends, so that we sometimes played together outside school, I know few more facts about Barbara's life than I do about the others. If you drew a line north from where we were photographed, continued it for a few miles out of town, it would take you to the crossroads on the way to the airport where Barbara's father was killed in a car accident shortly before she was born. Rule a line south from where we were grouped together at the front of the school, follow it for only a hundred yards or so, and you'll come to the nursing home where her elderly mother was living at the time of Barbara's death. Rule a line east for maybe a quarter of a mile and it leads to the house where she and Barbara used to live, with an aviary in the garden where Barbara bred budgerigars. And not far from there is the house Barbara lived in with her husband and children. No doubt the trajectories of most of our classmates will have crossed and recrossed the small area bounded by these lines, creating their own particular variations on the human story. Some will have stayed in the locality all their lives. A few, like Harry, will have gone much further afield. The toxic influence of the Troubles will have prompted many, like me, into exile "across the water" in Scotland, Wales, or England.

* * *

I wonder sometimes how many other copies of the Transition photograph survive. Every member of the class will probably have bought one, or maybe more, and the school's archive will surely have retained a copy. When they're looked at by others, as at least a few must surely be every now and then, I wonder what memories are triggered as the rows of faces are scanned. No doubt to some I will appear now as a stranger, my name forgotten, all memory of me vanished. It will be to them as if I'd never been there. Particularly since I moved away from the locality and lost touch with my old classmates, I'm curious about what happened to them. Looking at the photograph is a bit like finding a half-read novel that's been cast aside and forgotten about.

Rediscovering it years later, the hazily remembered narrative pulls me back into its world, makes me want to know how things unfolded, how the stories ended.

But though I'd like to know what happened in the futures of the people pictured, discover what happened next, find out beyond the odd snippet of news and rumor how life turned out for them in the years that followed as they left school and transitioned into adulthood, I'm more interested in the journey we all made to get to the moment when our class was photographed. I don't mean the little journey made to get to school on time that day, how we woke up, washed, got dressed, breakfasted, and left, following whatever unremarkable routine structured our lives back then. I have in mind our longer journey. Not just the one—incredible enough—from conception, to infancy, and through seven years of childhood to that moment of being photographed, but the odyssey of the bloodline we are part of, the way we each represent far longer lifelines than our own brief moments of warmth and blood and breath. Alongside the little calibrations by which we mark our days run millions of years of evolution; we're part of a genealogy that stretches back for distances that dwarf our mundane measures, integral parts of the trajectories that have borne us through eons.

Think of the transitions that are written into us, without which we wouldn't be here: from nothing to something; from inert to living; from single-celled beginnings through an array of multicellular organisms; from sea to land; from rudimentary nervous systems to brains sparkling with a multitude of neurons; from muteness to language; from silence to sentience. Each epochal transition is part of the chain of stepping stones our bloodline followed. If any step had not been taken, we'd not be in the photo. To be there—to be here today, writing about this astonishing journey—is dependent on a mesh of events of such scale, duration, and complexity it's hard to picture or properly appreciate the extent to which contingency creates us at every step along the way.

* * *

The more I think about what's contained within the neat rectangle of the photograph's plain black frame, the more the balance seems to shift, so that what's pictured is eclipsed by what it represents. The tip of the iceberg of our momentary appearance, what's obvious to the eye, points to the huge mass of time that's bulked in millions of years below the present's waterline. Behind the twenty-six bodies assembled here, the familiar forms we recognize and name, lies the story of their origin and nature, what those before us traversed so that we could arrive at the transience of our lives and be pictured at this passing moment. The imagination balks at what we stand for, our nature beyond the reach of lens and frame.

For a moment I think of the moving photographs in the Harry Potter books and toy with the idea of something similarly strange: not just people moving in and out of the picture, smiling, scowling, or waving to the viewer, but our likenesses caught in an altogether different gear. I try to imagine what we might look like, how we would appear, if it were possible to catch us with a longer exposure, one that encompassed our footprint over time, the species imprint we are part of. What would it look like, how would we see ourselves, if we could picture the artery that runs from life's first emergence, through various creatures, to the early hominids, and then to us? Instead of the tiny water droplets of twenty-six individuals featured in the photo of my Transition class, this imaginary image would show an immense deluge, the tidal wave of precursors, the ancestors that brought us to our momentary patch of shoreline pictured in the photograph.

As the simple picture explodes into a different focus, as I glimpse what's really there, it occurs to me that somewhere in our education we might benefit from transition days, or transition events, that would smooth a way between the common coin of our quotidian awareness and the reality that underlies it. Could we recognize ourselves pictured in this different focus, or would the images seem as other, as separate from us, as photos taken in infancy can appear in old age? We need something to mediate between the superficial scale of the everyday with which we customarily measure our lives and the scale of the canvas on which life's painted—in which we're embedded—something to gentle the transition between thinking in terms of days and months and years and the eons that have led to and lead away from them again.

* * *

When Miss Watt took the register in our Transition class, we were required to answer "Present" if we were there. If a register could be taken today, how many of us would still be present in the world? I know that two at least are not; they've passed into absence. And of course there may be others who have also made this transition. Or is death more a terminus, something that marks a cessation rather than any change or crossing, a bleak full stop that merely nullifies, the end of all transition? As Susan Sontag puts it, "Through photographs we follow in the most intimate, troubling way the reality of how people age." She sees photography as "the inventory of mortality." I know there will come a day, the change unmarked by any announcement, unnoticed by the world, when the last surviving member of my Transition class will take their final breath. Then none of us will be left. Who will this last survivor be? When and where will their inhalation falter, stop? What will be their final thought? And how long after thinking it before there's no one in the world who will recognize any of the faces in this portrait of my old Transition class, so that it becomes just another generic old photograph of unknown, vanished people, irrelevant to anyone living?

Particularly since there are twenty-six of us pictured, I can't help making the parallel with letters of the alphabet and wondering what our lives spell out. Does our existence constitute a script that does more than write "I was here" on the maze walls of our accidentalness? Whatever way we interpret the twenty-six hieroglyphs of being caught by the camera on that distant day, whatever sense we read out of (or into) this picture of ourselves, we should surely learn to recognize that though we left Miss Watt's class long ago, we're still in transition, with all the uncertainties and possibilities this entails.

When I think of where we've come from, where we're going, the paths we followed to the moment photographed and the paths we took away from it again, the photo's plain black frame seems inadequate for what's contained within it. What's pictured warrants something more akin to the way in which Tibetan *thangkas* are presented. These sacred pictures are designed as aids to meditation. They're intended as tools to further the great transition Buddhism is concerned with: moving us from an unenlightened to an enlightened state. Traditionally, *thangkas* are enclosed within boundary lines of red, yellow or gold, and sometimes blue. These painted frames are called "the rainbow" and serve as symbolic reminders of the realm of light out of which the enlightened beings who are portrayed have stepped to take physical presence here in the *thangka*. And such *thangkas* are often curtained to indicate reverence for what's there, to prevent casual, unreflective seeing, and to emphasize that what we're looking at is more a portal than a picture. Through it we can glimpse another realm of being beyond the curtailments of the everyday.

Of course I'm not suggesting that Miss Watt or any member of my Transition class was an enlightened being. That would be ridiculous. Nonetheless, I think it would be closer to apt than absurd to treat the photograph with the respect accorded to a *thangka*. Something like a rainbow frame and curtain would be fitting for what's pictured. At one level, of course, "an old photograph of my Transition class" describes this object well enough. There's nothing remarkable about it. But like so much of our ordinary vocabulary, there's also a sense in which such descriptions and the ballast of assumptions that they carry just don't fit what we affix them to. We learn them as labels necessary for everyday transactions. They get embedded in our diction and aid our routine fluency. But they also blinker, prevent us from seeing beyond the limited frame of reference that's sanctioned by convenience.

Look just a little closer and a powerful sense of mismatch will emerge as we start to realize how blindfolding common sense can be, how much it can prevent us from recognizing the true nature of our utterly remarkable, endlessly transitioning selves.

What Is It Like to be Alive?

The only information provided is in the caption: "A little boy with a horse in winter, 1958. Sweden." I first saw this photograph on December 6, 2017. That was the date when it turned up as the illustration on a calendar that gives a different picture for every day of the year. Since then, I've kept it by my desk and look at it often. In the way that some photos do, often for no apparent reason, this one speaks to me. It made an immediate impression; it continues to draw my eye, even though by now the elements of the picture are so familiar. For attribution, "Landskrona Museum Collection" is all that's credited. The name of the photographer isn't given.

What does the photograph show? A little boy is holding the reins of a white horse. They're standing in a snowy field or garden. There are four bicycles to his left. Only their rear wheels and saddles are visible; the photo cuts off the rest. The boy is holding the

horse's reins in his ungloved right hand. You can see his fingers clearly. His grip is too loose, and the disparity in size between boy and horse too great, for him to be exercising any real restraint or control. He's four years old at most. His left hand is empty and held relaxed by his side, encased in a thick woolen mitten. He's well-dressed for the cold: hat with earflaps tied snugly under the chin, heavy coat and trousers, boots. Apart from his right-hand fingers, the only exposed flesh is his face. He's looking toward the camera. It's hard to read his expression, but he seems content. The horse towers above him; the boy looks scarcely bigger than its head. It's a calm, unthreatening-looking animal, but to call it "placid" would be a misnomer; there's a powerful sense of strength implicit in its body, which seems massive in comparison to the boy. The horse's head is turned away from the camera, its attention taken by something out of the picture on the boy's right. Behind them are some leafless trees with snow-covered trunks and branches. It looks as if it's almost dusk, or perhaps it's just a heavily overcast day. It's snowing, and the camera has caught the pale smuts of numerous flakes as they fall earthwards. It makes it seem as if the sky is stippled with a scattering of blurred stars—and it's possible that at least some of what at first sight seem like snowflakes are indeed stars, their pale luminescence dappling the fading light. Boy and horse are standing on what is probably a path, partially cleared of snow. A pair of ski poles has been stuck into the ground not far behind them. It's hard to tell for sure, but the path may join a wider track or road. Where the ski poles have been planted could be part of the tree-lined bank that marks the edge of this thoroughfare, which looks as if it leads to a house. My guess is that the photographer was standing in its doorway, sheltered from the snow. Horse, boy, bikes, and ski poles, the suggestion of a path—there's something about the whole ensemble that has a sense of arriving home, even though no building is visible.

Describing the photograph is easy. It's more difficult to explain the impact that it has on me. It seems to have successfully caught a moment, which it offers up intact and perfect for the viewer to examine. It's almost as if a sliver has been netted from time's quicksilver flow and preserved here, its liquid voltage somehow confined within the frame, as if it were a kind of aquarium, instead of just draining away into the spent force of what's past. But almost any photograph can claim to capture whatever moment it pictures, albeit few do it as convincingly as this one. It's not this quality that gives the photo its particular potency.

What drew me to "A little boy with a horse in winter, 1958. Sweden"—and what keeps drawing me back to it—is the way it seems to pose a question and to propose itself as a contributory fragment of an answer. From the moment I saw the photograph on December 6, 2017, a question came with it. The same question accompanies it still. Whenever I look at the picture, I hear a voice asking: "What is it like to be alive?"

This is, of course, a metaphorical way of putting it. I don't mean I literally hear someone asking me this question. Hearing a voice that isn't there might cast aspersions on my sanity rather than explaining anything about the photo's impact. But the question has become so closely linked with the photograph that I can't look at it without its asking also happening. Naturally this won't be the case for everyone. Others will bring to their looking their own interpretive perspectives; they'll see the photo through the unique filter of the person they are. I can't tell what catalogue of associations this winter scene will create for others, or whether they'll find it as striking as I do. All I can say is that, for me, photograph and question have become so closely entwined that "What is it like to be alive?" now seems a better title for it than the one that's given.

Who poses the question? The best answer I can give is "The photograph itself." It's not as if the little boy—let alone the horse—turns questioner; it's not as if the ski poles or bicycles, the trees or snowflakes come emblazoned with this interrogation written on them so that everyone could see it. I don't think the lie of the land that's shown here has any question implicit in it, nor does the time of day or season. Yet there's something about the totality of this scene that sparks the question. Or maybe what I mean is that there's something about the totality of the encounter—of my seeing this image—that invariably results in the question being asked. Sometimes I try to picture what happens by thinking of the photograph's elements as swirling contour lines or isobars marking out the shapes of horse, boy, ski poles. When I look at them, these lineaments temporarily detach from their positions, uncoil from the shapes they mark out and snake into me, tangle with the lines of my inner topography. The intermingling that results before they return to the photo braids and knots the psyche so that this form of words is invariably thrown out: "What is it like to be alive?"

It is obviously an impossible question to answer—or at least to answer fully and conclusively. Maybe one of the things that keeps drawing me back to the photograph is the way the question beckons to itself a whole swarm of contributory answers. What is it like to be alive? It's like having the warm smell of horse in your nostrils as snowflakes fall on your face and melt there. It's like sitting writing this sentence, trying to choose words that convey my meaning. It's like the taste of sun-warmed wine, the feeling of thirst, the glint of candlelight on hair. It's like a pilot's view of runway lights, an egg hatching, a leaf falling. It's like feeling the bits of rust from an old anchor chain come off on your hands as you haul yourself aboard an abandoned fishing boat left beached in a remote bay. It's like being ambushed by a question held invisibly in a black-and-white photograph of a little boy holding the reins of a white horse.

I've tried out scores of formulations since first seeing the picture on December 6, 2017, and I know I'll try out more. But however large the swarm of answers grows, they'll never amount to more than a few droplets in a tiny rivulet that's one of billions feeding into an immeasurable ocean.

Who took the photo? The calendar gives no name. When I contacted Landskrona Museum, they told me that the photographer was Anders Hilding. This isn't the only Hilding photograph in their collection, but none speaks to me the way this one does. I can see the others are accomplished compositions, taken with a high degree of technical competence, often accompanied by considerable artistic sensibility. That's not surprising. Hilding was a respected press photographer. Born in Landskrona in 1931, his pictures appeared in the area's newspapers over a period of forty years. In 2007 the museum held an exhibition of his work. His pictures also appear in a series of books compiled by his friend and colleague Kalle Berggren. I'd like to have asked Hilding about the circumstances of his picture of the little boy and horse and wish I'd done so when I saw the photo in 2017. By the time I came to write this essay, it was too late. Hilding died in April 2020.

Looking at the museum's holdings also alerted me to the fact that Ven (formerly Hven) is within Landskrona Municipality. This is the island in the Øresund Strait where Danish astronomer Tycho Brahe (1546–1601) built Uraniborg and Stellaeburgum, his two famous observatories. I like to think of Tycho gazing into the same night sky the little boy in the photograph would have seen years later. What is it like to be alive? It's like lunar light falling on Tycho's retina, his brain forming pictures of the moon orbiting the Earth. It's like losing his heart to Kirsten Jørgensdatter, the commoner with whom he contracted a morganatic marriage, in accordance with the law at that time, alienating many members of his disapproving noble family.

And what of the little boy? I know nothing about him beyond what the photograph reveals. I don't know his name, where he lived, who his parents were. I don't know if he had brothers or sisters, whether he enjoyed school, what path he followed through the years, what gave him pleasure, what caused him pain. I don't know if he's still alive, but there's a good chance he is. Is there somewhere in Sweden today, drawing breath into his lungs as I write this sentence, the man in his sixties who the little boy grew up to be?

What is it like to be alive? It's like knowing there are lives glimpsed in passing that unfurl beyond my notice into whatever shape they take. It's like looking at a picture of Anders Hilding and knowing that the eyes you're looking at once looked at the scene framed in this photograph. It's like sailing beyond sight of land, feeling another's heart beat close to yours. It's like walking in the rain and shivering. It's like the recurrent knowledge of our certain death. It's like walking down a crowded city street or passing time with friends. It's like the sound of school playgrounds and the silence of the desert. It's like seeing injustice done and being powerless to prevent it. It's like the taste of cinnamon and blood and mint. It's like hearing a newborn's cries, watching news reports of famine, listening to an old man's fading breath. It's like balancing a tower of sea-polished pebbles till they fall, or throwing sticks for dogs.

Perhaps part of the appeal the photograph holds for me is that in 1958 I was about the same age as the little boy pictured. This makes me feel a kind of fugitive companionship, knowing that we've run life's course together, kept pace invisibly through the years without either of us realizing it, he following his life-story, I following mine, each locked into our own particular orbits of concern, members of a secret guild of unmet contemporaries, innocently complicit in the simultaneity of our momentary being. I imagine our two dots of sentient existence, the glow of our personalities, as tiny dust-speck meteorites following their trajectories across the space of our species' canvas, the biosphere of time and space that's occupied by *Homo sapiens*. What is it like to be alive?

It's like living amid the enormity of daunting numbers, knowing you're in the world with 7.8 billion unmet strangers, occupants of one planet among countless others in a universe that's some fourteen billion years old. It's like forging a niche of familiarity, a cocoon of home and family, amid incomprehensible scales of time and space. It's like knowing that in the end there's no image that can catch life's likeness, but simply the extraordinary reflection of our experiences looking back at us through the mirror of our consciousness.

In that most engaging of modern philosophical classics *Sense and Sensibilia* (1962), J. L. Austin makes an observation that always comes to mind when I look at Anders Hilding's photograph. Austin says that "like" is a "flexibility device," with whose aid, "in spite of our limited vocabulary, we can always avoid being left completely speechless." He sums up this point in a memorable image, suggesting that "like" provides the linguistic equivalent of being able to shoot around corners. The photograph's question seems to have taken Austin's valuation of "like" to heart. What gives "A little boy with a horse in winter, 1958, Sweden" its power is that it helps to avoid speechlessness when faced with the raw fact of Being. It encourages me to shoot around corners. Looked at directly, life shrugs off our attempts to net its nature or explain it. The obliqueness of the comparisons the photo prompts provides glimpses of fleeting meanings, elusive faces, glimmers of a sense of sense.

Splinter

It seems only fair to make clear at the beginning that I don't know how this story ends—or, rather, how it *will* end, for I've no reason to suppose it's not still unfolding. Elizabeth was only twenty-two when her life brushed against mine three years ago. The splinter that she left has taken this long to work its way to the surface, become something I can write about. Until recently it was embedded so deeply I couldn't reach it. Nor, if I'm honest, did I want to, given the poison it released anytime I tried. Now I want to close the forceps of words around it and attempt to pull it clear. What changed to make me feel I could finally get a grip on it? Maybe just the passage of time; maybe I've become desensitized. Whatever the reason, it has nothing to do with Elizabeth. She never realized that she left a splinter in me. I don't know how in the end she coped (or didn't cope) with the anguish in her life that dominated everything. I'm unsure if I acted correctly toward her. This is to stress that as well as not knowing its ending, the story I want to tell is one with many loose ends, uncertainties, and questions. An omniscient narrator I am not.

Let me hasten to correct the obvious misapprehension likely to be engendered by talk of one life brushing against another and leaving a splinter. I scarcely knew Elizabeth. We met together infrequently. We never touched. Our *relationship*—if that term can legitimately be used—was more professional than intimate. I only caught a glimpse of her story in the short period of her life I witnessed. I'd be surprised if she ever thinks of me now. My face is unlikely to surface in her memory in the way that hers still does in mine, tear-streaked and inconsolable. I'm sure she'd be astonished to discover how she became a kind of unwanted icon in my inner life, laden with the terrible burden she took on and posing questions I have no more idea how to answer now than I did when I first met her.

Two last points before embarking on the telling: first, the story is a true one, and I'll try to tell it honestly, though it reflects no great credit on me. What follows traces as accurately as I'm able the lineaments of that fragment of Elizabeth's life that got caught on my attention and memory. Others—Elizabeth most of all—would no doubt tell the story differently. Like any life-fragment, this one fractures the narrative light into a kind of starburst, creating a spectrum of rays; any of them could provide a storyline. How things appear on the page is rarely (is it ever?) the only way they can be seen. The circumstances of the particular entanglement of Elizabeth's life with mine, the way my own feelings intersected with hers, mean that this is my version of events, not how an independent witness would present them. However much I strive for truth, and I do, I know mine is a singular telling, one thread from that plurality of possibilities out of which we spin our take on the fabric of what happens.

The second point is simply to note that, in the now-expected manner of creative nonfiction, I've changed names and minor details in order to cast a protective membrane over those who might feel exposed by what I say. Given the correlation between the words on these pages and actual lives, rich with the complication of their feelings, I've extended the courtesy of protective obfuscation, drawing the literary equivalent of net curtains across identifiable clues of place and person. Or, to put a different spin on such apparently ethical authorial restraints, once hooded by anonymity, I'll feel less compunction about exposing on the page what others might prefer to keep hidden.

* * *

The basics of the story are easily enough set down, though its sharp needle point is hard to see at first, swathed as it is in particularities that are not at all dramatic. Elizabeth had taken one of my history courses. I knew her as a bright, hard-working student. Shy, almost to the point of being withdrawn, she was a quiet presence in classes, rarely offering any comment. Her written work was excellent, showing a depth of independent reading and a maturity of thought that was impressive. I was pleased when she elected to stay on after her first degree. For her doctoral dissertation she chose a topic that focused on some aspects of the Holocaust. This is a subject on which I have no specialist knowledge. I was surprised, therefore, when she emailed me to request a meeting.

I've always regarded it as a professional priority to be available to talk with students, particularly those in the early stages of research, when it's so easy to feel adrift. Establishing a good working relationship with a supervisor can be difficult. Some supervisors provide only minimal input; others are overdirective. Sometimes the change in gear from the more prescriptive ethos of undergraduate courses to the spirit of independent inquiry that characterizes postgraduate work causes problems. Not infrequently, new postgraduates simply feel lonely—research imposes a type of isolation that isn't met with in a first degree. It's often useful to talk things through with someone who understands the pressures but isn't directly involved in the emerging thesis, ideally a member of faculty other than a supervisor. This is something I encourage my own research students to do, and most of my colleagues are likewise happy to see their students seeking similar support, whether from me or someone else.

At our first meeting it became clear that simply in terms of practicalities, Elizabeth was floundering. She was getting almost no support from her designated supervisor, a newly appointed expert in the area but someone who, for all her internationally recognized standing as a Holocaust studies scholar, seemed close to clueless in terms of giving guidance about the nuts and bolts of putting together a piece of work on the scale of a PhD thesis. Of course research students need to work independently, but the situation Elizabeth described sounded more like abandonment than the skillful fostering of intellectual autonomy. I made some suggestions about structure and planning, and offered to read a thesis overview and draft introduction—stressing that I wasn't expert in the area and that it was imperative to seek her supervisor's input too.

At that first meeting I might almost have been lulled into thinking that Elizabeth's problems were ones commonly enough faced by novice postgraduates: feeling overwhelmed by the scale of the project they've undertaken; not knowing how to organize a manageable plan of work; having a sense of inadequacy, isolation, incipient failure—all aggravated by an absence of feedback. But as we talked it became clear that something far more problematic than such routine teething difficulties was troubling her. I could see that she was often on the verge of tears. It was only at our second meeting, when she was overwhelmed by them, that I began to see the real dimensions of what was wrong.

* * *

Ordinarily, one welcomes something close to obsession in research students. Unless their topic grips them in the vice of passionate engagement, unless their interest is intense, unless they're inwardly driven to spend long hours focused on the task, they're unlikely to produce work of the caliber expected at this level.

No one could have doubted Elizabeth's motivation or interest. She was consumed by her work. She showed the kind of single-mindedness and focus, the readiness to devote days on end to painstaking study that I would wish for any student hoping to write a successful doctoral thesis. That she had crossed the uncertain line separating interest from obsession might not have mattered much had she been working in another area. Such obsession can often be made light of as a kind of eccentric devotion, the harmless fanaticism that academic specialization sometimes kindles. In this instance, though, it was hard to put any such positive spin on it.

The thesis overview she produced was excellent: clear-minded, well informed, if maybe too ambitious in terms of what, realistically, could be achieved within the set limits of length and time. The draft introduction demonstrated a depth and breadth of reading that ring-fenced her topic within an impressive palisade of expertise. It also provided ample evidence of an incisive critical intelligence that could handle source material and competently evaluate competing interpretations of it. She wrote with the kind of confidence—authority—that only comes when high intelligence is paired with detailed knowledge. To my admittedly nonspecialist eye, she seemed fully in charge of her brief. I'm not a Holocaust scholar, but I've supervised enough PhDs to recognize a superb piece of work in the making.

As well as reading extensively, Elizabeth had visited Auschwitz and other Holocaust sites during her vacations. In addition, immediately after completing her first degree, she had spent several months working in a Holocaust museum near where she lived. Was she not the perfect student? At first I thought so, envied my colleague who was supervising her, and cursed the slipshod way in which she seemed to be handling Elizabeth's work. But the more I talked with Elizabeth, the more uneasy I became. My concern was pastoral, not academic. She was unquestionably brilliant—one of the brightest students I've ever come across. But her research was acting like a slowly cumulative poison. Here was someone whose work, for all the passionate interest and commitment she brought to it, had become a source of anguish rather than fulfillment. In the end, after several tearful sessions, I urged her to consider a different topic or to abandon research altogether. I'm still not sure if that was the right advice to give.

* * *

How much should we school ourselves in horror? To what extent is it incumbent upon us to be aware of history's atrocities? Specifically as regards the Holocaust, how much should we know about it? Are we duty-bound to educate ourselves and others in the causes and consequences of this most appalling act of evil, a crime that disfigured the twentieth century? Should we all, like the thirty million who have already done so, make the pilgrimage to Auschwitz-Birkenau, a kind of ethical hajj laid down as an obligation upon every citizen? Or, as time moves on, should we eschew such dark tourism, allow our attention to focus elsewhere—on the world's present ills—and let Auschwitz incline more to an important footnote in our consciousness rather than the banner headlines in which Elizabeth was painting it?

I'd considered such matters long before Elizabeth showed up in my office, wounded to her core by the work she was doing. Both for my own part, and as a parent thinking about how much children should be told and when, I'd pondered these difficult issues, albeit in a haphazard, nonsystematic way, and without arriving at any very definite answers. It seems important, certainly, to know something about the Holocaust. Ignorance of it would be tantamount to a kind of moral immaturity, even feeble-mindedness, and a parlous lack of historical perspective. On the other hand, to immerse oneself too fully in its detail, or to introduce children too early to the fact that it happened, would also be questionable. It's often said that those who don't remember the past are condemned to repeat it. It would be foolish indeed not to cultivate an awareness of how ordinary men and women are capable of visiting such cruelty on each other. But to allow the evil of the Holocaust to claim too much of our attention would also seem unwise. For my own part, I'd read some history, seen photos of the camps, and—by far the most significant input—listened to Primo Levi's unfailingly humane voice talking about the horrors that he'd witnessed.

With the Holocaust, as with so much else, there's no doubt an elusive middle way to strive for, a path that's balanced between too much and not enough—something that would allow us each to navigate a route such that understanding and empathy could flourish between the extremes of ignorance and overinvolvement. But plotting such a route is far from easy; exactly where it will lie upon the complex cartography of a life will vary from individual to individual. My meetings with Elizabeth made me think that while I was too close to ignorance, she'd embraced the pole of overinvolvement. If our meetings achieved anything positive for either of us, I like to think we were each nudged closer to a middle way.

* * *

Perhaps if she'd stayed at the level of facts and figures, tables of statistics, historical generalizations, an assessment of competing analyses and interpretations, it would all have worked out okay. Elizabeth's thesis might then have joined the scores of doctoral dissertations that stake out a territory whose boundaries are carefully marked by reference to already published work. She could then have proceeded to display a mastery of the minutiae within it, edging knowledge forward by adding some minuscule scraps of her own interpretation. Elizabeth was more than competent to produce work of this type. The problem was that she'd individualized the Holocaust: she saw its horror through the lens of particular people consumed by it.

For us now, in the early twenty-first century, "six million Jews were exterminated" has become a fact that, for all its enormity, can be fitted into the scheme of things; it's part of our historical perspective. It was seeing the faces of just three of these six million—a mother and her two children—that honed the usual statistic, blunted by its gross familiarity, into something of splinter sharpness. The protection of anonymous number was cut away to leave Elizabeth nakedly confronting the slaughter of the innocent.

It could, of course, be argued that to individualize the Holocaust, far from being problematic, is the correct way to view it. As Judith Miller argues:

> We must remind ourselves that the Holocaust was not six million. It was one, plus one, plus one.

Elizabeth had engaged in precisely this arithmetic, and it had moved her from scholarship into fathomless lament. “Holocaust Studies” might once have constituted her “field of research,” to whose burgeoning output of literature she could have added her own voice via a carefully written thesis. But her work had edged her into a depth of desolation no research could plumb or navigate. Though she was still trying to treat it as a “topic” when we met, it was clear to me that it had metamorphosed into something else entirely.

* * *

Appropriately for our image-dominated age, Elizabeth’s situation had come about because of a photograph. I can’t remember now where she found it, or the details of which death camp it pictured; perhaps she never said. She showed it to me at our third meeting, a folded copy taken from the back pocket of her jeans, creased with carrying and repeated lookings. It was a black-and-white photo of a mother and her two small children, a boy and girl of maybe eight and six. The mother is dressed in a dark shawl and long skirt—peasant-looking garb—and is carrying a suitcase. The children follow closely at her heels holding hands. The little trio looks harried, scared, completely vulnerable, but there’s nothing obviously horrific about the picture. It’s only when you learn that the photographer has caught them as they take their last steps on Earth that the image falls into a different declension. The building they’re approaching hides a gas chamber. In minutes this family group will be stripped, gassed, dead, their corpses burnt, their hair, clothes, shoes, and meager suitcase of possessions added to the grim mounds of material residue accumulated from the scores of others similarly annihilated.

Seeing the photograph had driven something deep into Elizabeth's psyche. It hit some fundamental nerve of decency within, splitting it asunder. As a result, one part of her kept replaying in her imagination the final paces of these three unmet—yet to her intimately known—strangers. In her imagination, Elizabeth walked beside the mother, sharing her repeated worried backward glances, reassuring the children, trying (hopelessly, she knew) to offer comfort. Another part of her searched frantically through the literature for reasons, explanations, and, most impossibly of all, something that might confer some meaning, something that might miraculously redeem, through an as-yet-undiscovered oasis, the pitiless desert of which this sand-grain image was, she knew, just one among millions of similar particles.

* * *

Meeting with Elizabeth, seeing her crying uncontrollably, listening to her—when the tears subsided—trying to explain how this image of mother and children left her feeling mesmerized and sullied, at once angry and distraught, I was reminded of some of Susan Sontag's comments in *On Photography*, her powerful meditation on the impact of images on contemporary sensibility. Sontag first saw images of the Holocaust when she was twelve years old and happened to stumble on some photographs of Bergen-Belsen and Dachau when she was browsing in a Santa Monica bookstore.

She describes such first encounters with the horror of the death camps as "the prototypically modern revelation: a negative epiphany" and says of her own encounter:

> Nothing I have seen—in photographs or in real life—ever cut me as sharply, deeply, instantaneously. Indeed it seems plausible to me to divide my life into two parts, before I saw those photographs and after.

Elizabeth's life seemed likewise to have been cut into two parts by the image of the doomed mother and her children that she carried folded in her pocket. How she was before and after seeing it were radically different states. Would it have been better for her never to have seen it? Or, having seen it, to have forgotten it before the image took such a hold of her? Are there things we should shield our eyes from? Or is there a moral imperative that demands we stare unflinchingly into the very heart of horror, however much anguish it may cause us? In the end, I advised Elizabeth to look away. Was that a betrayal of the mother and her little boy and girl, and of the millions they represent—a failure to keep faith with principled remembrance? Is choosing not to look an act of cowardice, even complicity, or can the deliberate embracing of ignorance sometimes claim to be compassionate and considered?

* * *

This photograph of mother and children on their way to the gas chamber had pierced Elizabeth like a splinter; a deadly sliver of dark mirror lodged in her flesh that kept on reflecting the same desolate scene, showing nowhere any glimmer of hope's light. It was as if she'd succumbed to a deadly enchantment. Yet this was no fairy story but something that witnessed to a terrible truth. Did it serve any useful purpose for her to be thus tormented?

Increasingly, I thought not.

While for Elizabeth it was a photograph that acted as a poisonous splinter, carrying the venom of the Holocaust deep into her bloodstream, for me it was Elizabeth herself. I don't know if she was Jewish; I don't ask students about their religion, and it wasn't something she ever volunteered. Whatever her faith, she came to represent for me a kind of archetypal victim: innocence abused and outraged. When her tearful face began to haunt me, its features seemed to bring with them a kind of distillate of the horrors she was studying. Her eyes held, and projected into mine, the terrible things she'd seen.

Does the fact that it was Elizabeth who touched me—not those actually slaughtered—suggest moral deficiency on my part? That I succumbed to a tearful young woman, rendered distraught by her thinking about their destruction, seems a dubiously secondary susceptibility. I only know that I came to see Elizabeth as a kind of living casualty of the Holocaust, someone threatened by the evil that still emanates from it—even at this remove of years. Brutally, honestly, the annihilated family was beyond anyone's help, but here was a living, breathing person who could be warned off the poison she'd uncovered.

Of course, we should never allow ourselves to forget what happened; we should take care to educate ourselves and our children about the camps; we should emblazon somewhere in our consciousness the key point made by Primo Levi:

> Whenever you begin by denying the fundamental liberties of mankind and equality among people, you move toward the concentration camp system, and it is a road on which it is difficult to halt.

But does such necessary awareness have to be bought at the price Elizabeth was paying?

* * *

Viewed in one light, Elizabeth's temporary placement in a Holocaust museum could be seen as a useful adjunct to her academic work. It brought a valuable new dimension into play, encouraging her to think about how information can be communicated by objects as well as words; how artifacts can be as potent harbingers of anguish as photographs or text. The fact that she was artistically as well as intellectually gifted meant she could give expert input into the design of exhibitions. She was alert to the nuances of display and had an instinctive grasp of what would work and what would not. I wasn't surprised that the museum had offered her a permanent curatorship, which she turned down in favor of continuing her doctoral research. I was surprised, though—shocked in fact—to discover the extent to which this Holocaust museum was keen to offer simulated experiences to the school parties that visited. To be crowded uncomfortably into a mock-up cattle wagon, wearing period costume, to listen to a tape of a moving train, to "arrive" at a destination where a recording of shouting guards was played, to be marched toward a darkened portion of a gallery meant to suggest a gas chamber, all the while surrounded by wall panels illustrating chilling scenes, seemed to me inappropriate, verging on the disrespectful. Does the mimicry of such playacting not risk undermining, albeit unintentionally, precisely the sense of shock and outrage that it wishes to inculcate? How can the routine replication of mere appearances do anything but weaken the sense of something so far beyond the pale of acceptable behavior that such facsimiles can't remotely reach it?

In my view, such ill-judged excess stands poles apart from the restrained approach exemplified by the way in which one small Holocaust exhibit is handled in Glasgow's St. Mungo Museum. The exhibit focuses on a prayer book used in a concentration camp near Auschwitz. As a backdrop to this book, a book that lures the eye, beckons the touch, because it has journeyed to hell and back, there's a collection of truly terrible black-and-white photographs. One of them shows a mass grave with figures about to be executed kneeling on its brink. The emaciated bodies, the murder about to happen, the seeming nonchalance of the executioners shock the eye. But these photographs are very deliberately displayed at a height that means that children are unable to see them. Only when they've grown in stature will they be able to look on such harrowing evidence of the evil we humans do.

In the ocean of images in which all of us now swim, it would be unrealistic to expect such care to be taken over every shocking scene that appears before us. Nor do the Internet, TV, newspapers, magazines, and other purveyors of the insistent images that minute by minute compete for our attention admit of such strategies of restraint as the simple expedient of elevation. Despite such difference, the skillfully placed photographs at the St. Mungo Museum raise hard questions about what we should notice and what we should avert our eyes from. At what point in an individual's life is it appropriate to look at the raw evidence of genocide? How can we avoid turning pictures of the dead or dying into casual icons of suffering, icons so routinely presented that they become pictorially commonplace and thus dismissible?

Susan Sontag suggests that "the omnipresence of photographs has an incalculable effect on our ethical sensibility" and warns that "living with the photographed images of suffering" may "not necessarily strengthen conscience and the ability to be compassionate. It can also corrupt them." Were Elizabeth's conscience and compassion being honed and strengthened by her preoccupation with that photo of the unknown mother and her children, or were they being damaged? I took the latter view and couched my advice accordingly.

* * *

If she had to fixate on a photograph of the Holocaust, I wish Elizabeth had chosen a different one. Susan Moeller is surely right in her claim that "images have authority over the imagination." Elizabeth's imagination was being ruled by something that was completely without hope. Her chosen icon fostered a despairing loss of faith in humanity. Perhaps if she'd been captivated instead by George Rodger's famous photograph *1945, Belsen, a Dutch Jewish boy walks through the camp*, she'd at least have been thrown a lifeline. It is another dreadful image, of what Rodger refers to as "the ultimate in human degradation," showing a young boy walking along a rough dusty track, beside which scores of emaciated, rag-clad corpses are strewn among the trees. He looks straight ahead, squinting slightly in the sun, gazing toward the camera. But the gross evidence of evil that appalls the gaze can at least be leavened by the knowledge that Sieg Mandaag, the boy pictured, was reunited with his remaining family after his aunt saw Rodger's photograph in *Life* magazine and recognized her nephew. There was no such glimmer of hope in the image that had so completely claimed Elizabeth's attention. Nothing could be salvaged from it.

* * *

If I were an omniscient narrator, if this were an imaginary story, if Elizabeth were a made-up character, I'd be able to bring things to a point of resolution. Perhaps her anguish would eventually overwhelm her, edge her into madness, even suicide. Or, were I given to inventing happier endings, she might fall in love, get pregnant,

find fulfillment in family life, and gradually forget about her demons. Or therapeutic distraction might come in the form of an enriching professional life that engaged her considerable intellectual and artistic talents in a career quite unrelated to Holocaust Studies. Or—a tougher challenge for a narrator—she might be presented as somehow discovering that elusive middle way between ignorance and overinvolvement.

As an essayist trying to trace out the contours of what happened and understand its moral topography, I have to rest content with loose ends, uncertainties, and questions—the lie of the land as it is rather than the geography of invention. A few months after discovering Elizabeth's plight, I moved to another job, sold my house, settled in a different country. The emails that passed between us became sporadic, then petered out altogether. I lost touch with colleagues at the university who could have reported on her progress. I don't know what she decided to do or how, if at all, she brought her research on the Holocaust into a less damaging alignment with her life. Perhaps Elizabeth's imagination is still held prisoner, caught under the authority of the image that tormented her. It's possible that she continues to struggle tearfully with her terrible icon, and that its poison will indeed destroy her, wrecking career, relationships, and any hope of ordinary, quotidian contentment. I hope instead that she's somehow learned to come to terms with what she made herself witness and moved on from where she was when I last saw her—even if this has meant discontinuing her studies and turning away from, learning to forget, the image that so obsessed her.

For myself, I'm less haunted now by Elizabeth than previously. Writing about her has helped, but the splinter that she left has by no means been expelled completely. I suspect it never will be. But I'm no longer sure if this is something I desire. Perhaps I need to accept its intermittent needling, learn to see it not as an unwanted barb but, rather, a necessary goad to keep on pricking my conscience, nudging me closer to responsible information and away from the default position of ignorance and forgetfulness to which, like almost everyone, I'm susceptible. But even as I write this sentence, a voice intrudes into its attempt to reach a neat conclusion. I can hear Elizabeth calling into doubt the possibility of ever finding balance when it comes to handling such extremes; she questions the morality of any middle way through the enormities that sparked her anguish. To my too comfortable notion of "a necessary goad" I know what her response will be. I see her take a worn piece of paper from the pocket of her jeans. She unfolds it for the umpteenth time, holds it up, looks at me accusingly.

Nicholson's Horses

There are many ways of seeing the same thing.

That's surely so obvious it's not worth stating. Readers might be forgiven for wondering what other truisms I'm going to follow this one with. Will I proceed to tell them that day follows night, that the earth is round, that we're all mortal? Yet though it may seem as much a statement of the obvious as these examples, my opening line has a different quality to it. It may appear self-evidently true, but it's often an uncomfortable truth that people don't want to live with. Rather than resting content with a diversity of views, we often like to privilege our own.

In suggesting that in the case I want to examine it's preferable to acknowledge a range of viewpoints rather than allowing any one of them the exclusive right to frame our outlook, I'm not sug-

gesting that any way of seeing, this one included, is exempt from criticism. All of them should be kept open to scrutiny. But we need always to ensure that the process of judgment is sensitive (but not subservient) to context.

The thing I want to look at is a statue. It features a larger-than-life-sized bearded man in bronze. He's in military-looking garb and stands on a granite plinth. His pose is warlike. His right arm is raised, holding a sword. There's a pistol in his left hand. It's as if he's been plucked straight from the midst of battle and set down here, frozen in warrior pose. His ferocity is incongruous amid the humdrum scenes around him. The statue is located in a city center square, surrounded by the bustle of traffic and pedestrians.

A sword-wielding, pistol-pointing giant of a man may sound eye-catching. Surely everyone would notice it. Perhaps that's so initially. At first encounter, such a threatening depiction is almost bound to leave a strong impression. But for me, familiarity has disarmed it, blunting the sword's edge, emptying the pistol's bullets, shrinking the man's massive stature. His figure has been brought within the fold of what's recognized, accustomed, scarcely noticed. The statue has become part of the everyday signature of the place in which it's standing. Despite its weaponry, it makes me think of home, not battle. Far from any association with bloodshed, it brings to mind memories of a peaceful childhood.

Looking at a photograph of the statue now, as I write these reflections—hundreds of miles away from where it's standing—I'm hard-pressed to recall anything about the man depicted, though I've walked past his belligerent form countless times. Instead, I remember my childhood fascination with the curious folds in the cloth that drapes the back of his neck. This cloth is an integral part of the peaked cap that the sculptor has shown him wearing. I'd never seen anything in this style before and was much struck by it. It's designed to protect its wearer from the sun. I was intrigued by how pliability, even softness, could be suggested in such a rigid material as bronze.

At this point in my life, the statue acts as a kind of hook, baited with the memories of childhood. Looking at the photograph I'm reeled back through the years. There I am, a small boy walking hand-in-hand with his mother. She has a wicker basket in her other hand; clearly we've been shopping. As we pass the statue, I look for the familiar marker, ticking off in my mind those intriguing folds on the neck flap.

Sometime in those distant days, I asked my mother who the man with the sword was. The only thing I recall from what she said was the name "Nicholson." Whether that was all she told me, or all that I remembered, is impossible to establish now. My mother died in 2007. I wish I'd thought to ask her what she knew about the statue, how she saw it, what it meant to her. Might she even have been present at its unveiling? For me, the statue has always been there. It's just one of the well-worn contours of home, an established landmark of the town where I grew up. It's part of a familiar pattern I recognize instantly. But my mother might just have been able to remember a time before it was there. It was erected in 1922, when she was five years old.

Perhaps, walking hand-in-hand with her mother, she went past this newly installed figure and, echoing my question to her decades later, asked who the intimidating man with the sword and gun was. Would her mother have been able to tell her any more than a name? Information about it apart, the statue probably acted for her, as it did for me, as a repository of memories, a grid reference for personal associations. Perhaps it was somewhere to meet friends, a conveniently central point in town that was unambiguously identifiable: "I'll see you at seven by Nicholson's statue." I like to think of little assignations of friendship and courtship unfolding in the shadow of the grim figure on the plinth. And, like me, my mother may have been struck by some seemingly unimportant aspect of the statue. Maybe instead of the folds on the neck drape, she fixated on Nicholson's long boots, or the cut of his jacket, or the tassel shown dangling from the handle of his sword, an incongruously dandyish addition to his warlike stance, something that would be more in place decorating a curtain-tie in some genteel drawing room than affixed to the hilt of a no doubt often bloodied blade.

Beyond whatever idiosyncratic points of reference it may have had for her, my guess is that my mother didn't know anything about who Nicholson was, or what he'd done, or why a statue of him had been erected here. She never had much time for history.

There are many ways of seeing the same thing.

The Nicholson statue is in the center of Lisburn, a Northern Irish town (a city since 2002) eight miles southwest of Belfast. Nicholson is John Nicholson (1822–1857). Though born in Dublin, he had strong family connections with Lisburn. His mother, Clara Hogg, was born there. She and Nicholson's father, Alexander, were married in Lisburn's Church of Ireland cathedral in 1820. The cathedral's doors are just a stone's throw from the statue. As they left the marriage ceremony—was confetti thrown, or rice, to wish them luck?—they could never have imagined that a century later the son they kindled, loved, protected would be memorialized here, so close to where they stood, each one rapt in the private awareness of their nuptials and thoughts of what lay ahead.

Alexander Nicholson was a doctor. He studied medicine in Dublin and, once qualified, worked there. After his early death (he contracted a fatal illness from one of the patients he was treating) Clara and her seven children moved back to Lisburn. At that point John was only nine. If he had lived to see it, would his father have been proud or ashamed of the man his son became? We are all creatures of our own times and the values they instill in us. Parents have a tendency to overlook—or forgive—their children's flaws. It's entirely possible that Alexander Nicholson would have seen his son in the glowing terms of approbation Victorian Britain accorded him. But I can't help wondering if, as a doctor, concerned with the saving of lives, he might have looked askance at John's death-dealing adulthood. Would he have seen his child as brave, heroic—someone matured into a man of principle, honor, and courage? Or would he have seemed brutal and brutalizing, a monster of a man who killed casually, seemingly without compunction?

John Nicholson didn't remain in Lisburn long. At the age of twelve he was sent to the Royal School, thirty-five miles away in Dungannon, County Tyrone. Four years after that he left for

England, where he stayed briefly with an uncle before sailing for India in the employ of the East India Company. On arrival, after basic training, Nicholson served as an ensign in native infantry regiments. From these modest beginnings he rose through the ranks and became an administrator as well as a soldier. He saw action in Afghanistan, and in Kashmir, Peshawar, and other parts of India. In 1847, he became assistant to Sir Henry Lawrence, Resident at Lahore. He served for several years as governor of the Punjab. By 1857 he held the rank of Brigadier-General. In September of that year, Nicholson led the British attack that recovered Delhi during the First Indian War of Independence, still known in my schooldays as "the Indian Mutiny." In the course of an assault on the city's Kashmir Gate, Nicholson was shot. He died of his wounds nine days later, at the age of thirty-five. The statue depicts him in the heat of that last fatal battle, shortly before he fell.

In *Cult of a Dark Hero: Nicholson of Delhi* (2018), Stuart Flinders describes the day of the statue's unveiling in 1922:

> Lisburn came to a standstill as shops, schools and factories closed for the event. The Prime Minister of Northern Ireland looked on as a former Chief of the Imperial Staff, Field Marshal Sir Henry Wilson, a Unionist MP, led the ceremony. The statue, he told the crowd, was to be seen not only as something to be "intensely proud of but as something sacred" and he urged them "to teach your children the story of the life of John Nicholson of Lisburn."

There are many ways of seeing the same thing.

Seeing the statue as "something sacred" could, if taken literally, lead to the kind of idolatry that no doubt Wilson and his audience would have condemned. I suspect that what Wilson had in mind when he said this wasn't the man himself but the values he thought Nicholson represented. If asked to specify the values people should see as "something sacred," a man of Wilson's time, class, and rank would probably have stressed service, duty, honor, courage, loyalty to King and country, self-sacrifice, discipline, and adherence to the orthodoxies of Christian faith. Undoubtedly, Nicholson possessed some of these qualities. There's no denying his bravery, for example. But it would be hard to square many of his actions with the teachings of Jesus. His ferocity inclined more to fire and the sword, vengeance and retribution, than to anything approaching love and forgiveness. Most people today would be appalled by some of his beliefs and by the violence he meted out. Even for an audience in 1922, Nicholson's attitudes might have seemed extreme. Learning of the deaths of European civilians during the fighting in 1857, Nicholson suggested to a fellow officer:

> Let us propose a Bill for the flaying alive, impalement, or burning of the murderers of woman and children at Delhi. The idea of simply hanging the perpetrators of such atrocities is maddening. . . . A few years ago men (frequently innocent) used to be tortured merely on suspicion. Now there is no punishment

> worse than hanging, which is a very easy death. . . . We have different scales of punishment for different kinds of theft, assault, forgery, and other crimes—why not for murder?

Ironically, given what Field Marshal Sir Henry Wilson said at the unveiling about the statue representing "something sacred," Nicholson himself came to be revered. While he was alive, Nicholson was declared an incarnation of the god Brahma by a Hindu holy man, and small groups of devotees began to treat him as an object of devotion. Nicholson wasn't impressed. On several occasions he had members of this unlikely cult flogged when he considered their adulation had overstepped the mark. In his 1939 biography of Nicholson, *The Hero of Delhi,* Hesketh Pearson records that on learning of Nicholson's death, two of the leaders of this so-called "Nikolseynite" cult "cut their throats and were buried in the graves they had made before committing suicide." Remarkably, belief in Nikal Seyn as some kind of demigod survived his death and even continued into this century. Stuart Flinders offers these comments on a sect that no one in that Lisburn crowd in 1922 is likely to have heard of:

> Its original followers were described sometimes as Hindus, sometimes as Sikhs. However, after Nicholson's death the cult was taken up by Shi'a Muslims in remote parts of the Punjab. Stories of Nicholson bringing peace, justice, and, where nec-

> essary, retribution merged with ancient tales from Islam and he became a mystical figure, part folk hero, part Muslim legend. Changes in population and traditions of religious practice saw the cult's gradual decline throughout the twentieth century. It was kept alive in Abbotabad (in present-day Pakistan) by a family that took care of the Christian cemetery there. The caretaker's job and the stories of Nikal Seyn were handed down through the family to Ali Akbar, the last of the Nikal Seynis, who died in 2004.

There are many ways of seeing the same thing.

I don't know if anyone in that Lisburn crowd in 1922 took Wilson's words to heart and really did see Nicholson's statue as something to be "intensely proud of," "something sacred." But I do know that by the time I was growing up in Lisburn a few decades later, neither I nor any of my contemporaries knew anything about the statue beyond the fact that it was there and that it depicted someone called Nicholson. I don't ever remember its being mentioned at school, still less made the subject of a lesson. I fear the Field Marshal would have been dismayed by how quickly the story he wanted children to know faded from public attention. Until I came to write this essay, *Nicholson* was just a name, his statue of no more (or less) importance than the familiar buildings and roads surrounding where it stands.

My brother and I were raised in Lisburn and lived there until early adulthood. Then the Troubles, university, jobs, and marriage led to our settling "across the water." We're now only infrequent visitors to our old hometown. Writing about the Nicholson statue made me wonder about my brother's impressions of it. How does he remember it at this stage in his life? Predictably, his level of ignorance about Nicholson matches mine. What surprised me was that he remembers the statue as an equestrian one, with Nicholson astride a rearing horse. My wife likewise pictures Nicholson thus, remembering a horse that was never there. This is less surprising. She didn't grow up in Lisburn. For her, the statue is a recently encountered phenomenon rather than part of the underlay of childhood. For my brother, as for me, the statue is something ingrained into the tread of the accustomed, a tread that laid its weight on us for years. Yet we've remembered this little detail of the catechism of home in significantly different ways.

The statue of Nicholson unveiled in Lisburn in 1922 shows the single figure of a standing man. There is no horse. To see one is an error in recall, a misremembering, something the mind has fabricated or taken from elsewhere. Where did the horses come from that trotted into my brother's and my wife's recollections of Nicholson? If they'd known anything about the man, it would have been a reasonable enough addition. Nicholson spent a lot of time on horseback during his postings to Afghanistan and India. Indian railways were in their infancy in Nicholson's lifetime, with the first passenger train only appearing in 1853. Pre-train, the horse was an essential adjunct for the numerous administrative and military tasks that he performed. The *Dictionary of Ulster Biography* records that in one of the battles he fought in, Nicholson "was said to have been in the saddle for twenty hours." But since neither my wife nor brother knew anything about Nicholson beyond his name, their horses weren't introduced into the picture by reasonable extrapolation from his biography. Rather, I think they simply remembered the statue as something martial and then confused it in their minds with military statues seen elsewhere, where the subjects are indeed shown mounted. After all, a rearing warhorse is quite in keeping with a brandished sword and pistol.

Seeing Nicholson on a horse is mistaken in an unproblematic way. It's easily corrected. Simply look at the statue itself, or a photograph of it, and it's instantly apparent no horse is there. It's the less obvious misapprehensions that are concerning: Nicholson as hero; Nicholson as savior; Nicholson as someone we should honor and emulate; Nicholson as protagonist of a story we should tell our children; Nicholson as an embodiment of values that should be remembered, admired, considered sacred. Such ways of seeing are in my view as mistaken as seeing him astride a horse. But they are more insidious, harder to correct: simply looking at the statue won't dispel them.

There are many ways of seeing the same thing.

What made me think of Nicholson's statue again, all these years after leaving Lisburn? He came back to mind because of another statue, one that hit the headlines in the UK in the summer of 2020. On June 7 of that year, a statue of Edward Colston in

Bristol was torn down by protestors and dumped in the city's harbor. Colston (1636–1721) had previously been honored as a generous benefactor. He provided funds for hospitals, schools, and churches. The statue, by Irish sculptor John Cassidy, included this inscription on the plinth: "Erected by citizens of Bristol as a memorial to one of the most virtuous and wise sons of their city, AD 1895." For many years, this bronze figure of Colston was a familiar landmark in the city center.

By the 1990s, Colston's reputation as an epitome of virtue and wisdom was contested. As his involvement in the slave trade became increasingly apparent, *philanthropist*—at least without careful qualification—started to look like a misnomer. Spurred by the Black Lives Matter movement, and the protests surrounding the murder of George Floyd in Minneapolis, some of Bristol's citizens decided to take direct action. The statue was defaced, toppled, dragged to the quayside, and thrown in. I watched the news coverage of this event. But it was an email from a friend in Bristol that turned my thoughts from Colston to Nicholson. She wrote to say that though she was sympathetic to the protestors and shared their sense of anger and injustice, she was saddened to see the statue pulled down. She didn't think of Colston as either a benefactor or a beast. The bronze statue simply acted as an important marker of her childhood, a feature of the area in which she'd been raised. In particular, the statue had fond associations for her of time spent with her father. They sometimes stopped beside it to eat ice cream. The protestors saw the statue as honoring a man who had been involved in something irredeemably vile. For my friend, it was a familiar feature of her world, swathed in cherished personal recollections. What she said made me think of walking past Nicholson's statue with my mother. To me, it's a fondly remembered landmark, part of the familiar fabric of my childhood. But is it also, like Colston's statue, a representation of something odious?

There are many ways of seeing the same thing.

Nicholson was lauded as "the saviour of Delhi" and became a popular hero of empire in Victorian Britain. In *The Life of John Nicholson: Soldier and Administrator* (1900), Lionel James Trotter notes how "the heroic Nicholson" is "the title by which the men in his own generation love to speak of this young soldier-statesman." Trotter presents a picture of Nicholson as a paragon of complementary virtues. He talks about his "iron will" and "strong sense of duty," of his being a magistrate who was "terrible to evil-doers." But Nicholson also possessed "the tenderness of a woman" and "the thoughtful kindness of a true gentleman." A similar panegyric is offered in R. E. Cholmeley's *John Nicholson: The Lion of the Punjab* (1908). As a "soldier, administrator, and leader of men," says Cholmeley, Nicholson "ruled wisely and well." He presents the subject of his book as a "high-minded, pure-souled" individual who lived "cleanly and righteously." His death, accordingly to Cholmeley, "created a sense of national loss."

Given this kind of status, it's not surprising that a statue was erected. Nicholson's family connections with Lisburn (though he wasn't born there, despite what it says on the statue and in Trotter's and Cholmeley's books) meant that people wanted to emphasize links between this heroic personage and their town. But there was more to the timing and placing of the statue than civic pride or memorialization. In 1922, Northern Ireland was freshly separated from the rest of Ireland. Most of the country was in Eire, the new Free State; only six counties remained tied to Britain. Unionist identity needed bolstering. What better icon of imperial belonging—rather than Irish independence—than an image of John Nicholson? The statue was gifted to the town by a local man, Henry Musgrave. It was made by F. W. Pomeroy (1856–1924), one of the most eminent sculptors of the time, whose prolific output includes the figure of Justice at the Old Bailey in London.

If Protestant sensibility in Lisburn, as elsewhere in Northern Ireland, was governed by a siege mentality, here was a tangible source of succor, a kind of battle standard of Britishness erected in the loyalist heartland. With his raised sword and pointing gun, Nicholson's statue helped steel the nerve of a beleaguered minority. Just as he'd taken arms against rebellious natives in Delhi, braved fearful odds, and secured victory, so could they withstand any "mutiny" that might ignite around them here.

There are many ways of seeing the same thing.

Finding examples in Nicholson's life of things we would condemn isn't difficult. For instance, in *The Last Moghul* (2006), William Dalrymple quotes an incident recorded in the diary of one of Nicholson's fellow officers, Lieutenant Edward Ommaney.

Ommaney writes that Nicholson "thrashed a cook boy for getting in his way. The boy complained, he was brought up again, and died from the effects of the second thrashing." There are well-documented cases of Nicholson ordering the summary execution of prisoners. To ensure law and order in one of the areas of India he was charged with administering, he took direct action against an outlaw chief who had been terrorizing local villages. He rode to where the man was known to be quartered, in the midst of his kinsfolk, engaged him in single combat, and killed him. He then decapitated the corpse and kept the head in his office as a way of discouraging other marauders. On another occasion, discovering a plot to poison him and his guests, he simply delayed dinner while he had the cooks hanged. On the battlefield he led from the front. In the thick of the fighting, he used sword and pistol expertly and without mercy. The Lisburn statue is no romanticized pose, it pictures Nicholson's modus operandi as a warrior.

An indication of his lethality in action can be gleaned from John Kaye's assessment in *Lives of the Indian Officers* (1889). He suggests that "Nicholson is an army in himself." Half a century later, in *The Hero of Delhi*, Hesketh Pearson writes:

> His was the Old Testament method of dealing with enemies and he did not expect the man he was disembowelling to respect his feelings as a gentleman. He admired the Christian virtues, but they were foreign to his nature and made him uncomfortable. 'Smite or be smitten' was his guiding principle in life.

Clearly, Nicholson committed many acts that, were they done today, might see him charged with war crimes, or with serious civil offenses. Morally, some of his behavior is beyond the pale of anything our twenty-first-century sensibility would find acceptable. His frequent brutality is undeniable, as is what Donal McCracken calls his "furious and frightening temper." But McCracken is uneasy about simply condemning Nicholson in the outright manner of William Dalrymple, who refers to him as "this great imperial psychopath." McCracken sees a shy, lonely man, probably a repressed homosexual, who was beset by inner demons. As well as the psychological scarring from his father's early death and growing up in straightened circumstances in "a gloomy puritan household," ruled over by a "religiously fixated" mother, his experience as a very young man of conflict in Afghanistan and India was traumatic and brutalizing. In *Nicholson: How an Angry Irishman Became the Hero of Delhi* (2018), McCracken also advances the theory that some of his subject's more extreme behavior may be partially attributable to medicines he was taking, in particular what he describes as "the nineteenth-century cure-all 'blue pill.'" Mercury, linked with unpredictable and violent outbursts, was a major ingredient in this supposed panacea.

There are many ways of seeing the same thing.

I hope I've not been unsympathetic to John Nicholson. It's easy to sit in judgment at this remove in history, to allow the present's sledgehammer certainties free rein to rampage through the past, order the summary execution of anything we disapprove of. Looking back can become an exercise in promoting a kind of procrustean perspective that mutilates whatever doesn't fit neatly into our twenty-first-century bed of values. In his time, in the places where he served, Nicholson was faced with brutalities and dangers that I wouldn't know how to deal with. He was routinely confronted by terrifying situations that I'd have run away from. I've no idea how I might have reacted if, like Nicholson, I'd discovered the naked, mutilated body of my brother after hostilities at the Khyber Pass. Witnessing such atrocity is unlikely to have led to any gentleness in his dealings with those he thought responsible. Who knows the impact on Nicholson's psyche of being held prisoner, almost sold into slavery, having assassins sent to kill him, witnessing extreme cruelty and violence on a regular basis? Though they may have been employed in dubious actions, Nicholson's courage, toughness, and sheer endurance were remarkable. In a tight corner he'd have been a good man to have on your side. And it's worth noting reports of villagers holding him in great esteem because he'd brought peace, order, a semblance of fairness into areas of vicious tribalism and lawlessness. His methods may strike us as unpalatable, but they were sometimes effective in ending the violent exploitation of the vulnerable.

There are many ways of seeing the same thing.

What should be done with Nicholson's statue? Should it just be kept as it is? Is it enough to surrender to the laissez faire of "It's been there for so long it's part of the place," allow that mere duration can defuse any unwelcome associations that may creep in as the facts of Nicholson's life come into clearer focus? Is it acceptable to argue that it's a historical document of sorts and should simply be preserved, intact and undamaged, testimony to a past that—whether we approve of it or not—we cannot change? Or should it be torn down à la Colston, dragged away, and dumped in the nearest deep water, in Lisburn's case the river Lagan? Would destroying it be symbolically therapeutic, help to distance us from what it represents, make clear we've moved on, have different values?

I'm not sure where my sympathies lie in this. I've come to regard the statue with an uneasy mix of nostalgic affection and revulsion. To try to satisfy both reactions, my preference would be for something that's unlikely to happen. It lacks the simplicity of the leave it or destroy it options, and my "solution" would also require time and money. I'd like to see the statue being pressed into service as an educational device. If we let it tell a more complicated story than the one Field Marshal Wilson had in mind at the unveiling, it could help drive home the truth I've been repeating: "There are many ways of seeing the same thing." But for it to do this effectively would mean, at the very least, adding some alternative captions to the plinth so that different interpretations of Nicholson could be laid before anyone who stopped to look. Ideally, it would also involve local schools addressing the matter, looking at the ways in which Nicholson can mean such different things at different times and to different people.

Imagine if Lisburn had another benefactor like Henry

Musgrave, offering to fund the commissioning of a new statue to put beside—or indeed replace—Nicholson's. Who would be the likely candidates? Henry Monro, perhaps? He was the Lisburn merchant who led local United Irishmen against British forces at the Battle of Ballynahinch in June 1798. The United Irishmen were defeated. As well as those who fell in battle, many innocent lives were lost as British troops, with considerable brutality, expunged any further inclination among the population toward rebellion. Monro was taken the seven miles back to Lisburn and hanged within sight of his own front door; his head was severed and put on a spike. This grisly disincentive to others was displayed in Market Square, where Nicholson's statue stands. One assumes that Nicholson would have applauded this piece of theatrical butchery.

Or might Lisburn's founder, Welsh nobleman Sir Fulke Conway, have a claim? King James I granted him a huge tract of land, known as Killultagh, in 1611. Conway chose the area of what would become Lisburn as the site of his fortified residence. But both these figures would be controversial. Unionists would regard Monro as a traitor; nationalists would view Conway as a colonial usurper who stole land belonging to an ancient Irish clan. Perhaps a less emotive choice would be Louis Crommelin (1652–1727), a refugee who was instrumental in setting up the manufacture of linen, an industry that did so much to shape the history of the town. But Crommelin was a Huguenot fleeing religious persecution in France, so instead of being viewed as a shared commercial icon he might be pressed into symbolic service by both sides in the local sectarianism that still divides Catholics and Protestants. Or what about the great theologian Jeremy Taylor (1613–1667), most famous for his books *The Rule and Exercise of Holy Living* and *The Rule and Exercise of Holy Dying*? No less an authority than Coleridge rated Taylor alongside Shakespeare, Milton, and Bacon as one of the great exemplars of seventeenth-century prose. Taylor held a post in Lisburn cathedral and died in the town in 1667. He's buried in nearby Dromara.

Or, instead of reaching back into the distant past, why not choose someone more contemporary? I'm pleased that this is what was done for the most recent statue in Lisburn. Outside the newly built civic center you'll find a bronze figure of physician and cardiologist Frank Pantridge, who was born nearby in 1916. He's honored as inventor of the mobile defibrillator. It's interesting to compare Pantridge and Nicholson. Sometimes Nicholson's behavior is explained, even condoned, by saying that he was surrounded by brutality. How else could he have acted in such circumstances? It's worth noting that Pantridge too experienced, in unwanted abundance, the cruelty that humans visit on each other. Perhaps the most striking thing about his memoir, *An Unquiet Life* (1989), is the contrast between the brutalities he encountered in wartime and the lifesaving initiatives he pioneered. As a medical colleague put it, "he saw thousands die cruel deaths, but he went on to restore to useful life, often full recovery, much greater numbers." When war broke out in 1939, Pantridge volunteered and was posted to Malaya as medical officer to an infantry regiment. His account of the fall of Singapore, and in particular the Japanese army's savage execution of the wounded in one of the island's hospitals, makes harrowing reading. Similarly grim are his recollections of being a POW working on the Siam–Burma railway. Many of his comrades perished, but Pantridge survived, despite contracting a serious illness and being sent to the notorious Tanbaya death camp. When he was liberated in 1945, he weighed just under five stone. But he recovered, continued his medical career, and became consultant physician at Belfast's main hospital. He died in 2004. I like the fact that the sculptor, John Sherlock, has included in his depiction of Pantridge an early prototype of the mobile defibrillator. To my mind this small, box-like object is worthier of memorialization than any raised sword or pistol.

There are many ways of seeing the same thing.

As I was working on this essay, a life-sized statue of Swedish environmental activist Greta Thunberg was installed on the University of Winchester's campus. It was instructive to see students' reactions. The overwhelming majority agree that Thunberg is an inspirational figure, someone to admire and respect. But they reckon it suggests a poor sense of priorities on the part of the university to invest considerable funds commissioning a statue of her. Why not spend the money on library provision, scholarships, or indeed donations to environmental charities? Do we need statues to remind us of the values we espouse?

My favorite statue of a historical person is the one of Montaigne in a shady square in Paris's fifth arrondissement, opposite the National Museum of the Middle Ages and facing the Sorbonne. Students believe that it's good luck to touch Montaigne's right shoe before an exam. The number of touches over the years has left that part of the statue with a brighter luster than the rest. Montaigne would no doubt have been amused by such superstition. His hope would have been that as well as touching his shoe students would attend to that key process of learning that he recommended for everyone, namely, that we should "rub and polish our brains by contact with those of others" (this from his essay "Of the Education of Children"). When it comes to thinking about statues, such contact should leave our awareness as polished as Montaigne's right shoe, bright with the recognition of there being many different viewpoints and the realization that some of the ideas, allegiances, and values they contain are as questionable as the nonexistent horses that don't support Nicholson on his plinth.

No doubt examples could be found in Montaigne's life and writings that we would condemn as racist, sexist, ageist, speciesist, or falling foul of our moral orthodoxies in some other manner. But a comment he made (in "Of Cannibals") is worth keeping in mind whenever we look at his—or any—statue: "Each man calls barbarism whatever is not his own practice."

There are many ways of seeing the same thing.

Images of Hallow Hill: Exploring the Meaning of a Place

For me, Hallow Hill has two images so closely bound to it that it requires a special effort to see past them to the reality of the place itself. The first one is, in part, straightforward. It pictures gleeful children sliding down the hill's gentle slopes on brightly colored plastic sledges. Bulky in their hats and gloves and insulated jackets, they clumsily run back up—the towed sledges pulled by cords knocking at their heels and sometimes making them stumble. But in my mind's eye I see them sledging not just on the shallow covering of snow with which Hallow Hill is periodically clad in winter, but on a surreal mix of snow and human bones. The white of skeletons jutting their hard angularity from the ground sounds a discordant note amidst the softness of the gently falling snowflakes. Many of the skeletons are children's, creating a shocking contrast as the sledging children weave their way around snow-rimed skulls and ribs and vertebrae that are no bigger than their own.

There's no mystery about the children. They're drawn from life. I've often seen them on Hallow Hill in winter; it's the best spot locally for sledging and so draws them like a magnet anytime it snows. But I've never seen skeletons here. To understand where they come from and why, for me, they characterize Hallow Hill just as much as sledging children, requires a brief excursion into history.

* * *

Before making that excursion, though, I want to sketch out the second image that's spliced and bound to my view of this place, doing much to determine how I see it. And before I do that I want to make sure that the obvious provenance of the sledging children, the bright primary colors suggested by their play, isn't allowed to diminish the skeletons. Since the skeletons aren't really there, since I've never seen them in the way I've seen the children, it would be easy to let the bones fade, become shadowy and indistinct, something merely imagined, eclipsed by the raw, urgent presence of the children in their cheerful winter clothes.

It's important to recognize that my image of the children isn't some superrealistic depiction beside which the bones are rendered secondary and subsidiary. In the crucible of memory and imagination, where skeletons and children have been forged together into a single image, each has equal value. It's not as if my picture of the children is like a finished portrait in which no detail has been omitted, while the bones appear only in spectral fashion as a shadowy and incomplete impression. When I stop to examine it, the way I see the sledging children approximates more closely to a mosaic that has many pieces missing. It's a patchwork of pieces drawn from memories that were laid down on different occasions. For all the apparent simplicity suggested by describing it as "children sledging in the snow," the image is something vaguer than a set of photographs held picture-perfect in the mind. None of the children's faces in my image is clear. I don't know how many of them there are or their names or ages, or whether there are more boys or girls. Details of their bright apparel are indistinct. If I try to focus on them, they dissolve into uncertainties.

In the same way, the soundtrack of shouts and cries and laughter is no faithful transcription of real utterance, contouring precisely the rise and fall of actual children's voices. Rather, it's a pastiche based on remembered noises and augmented by the imagination. *Image* can suggest something framed, precise, clear-cut. Closer examination suggests a far less definite—but no less powerful—thing. Since they exercise so strong an influence on my understanding of Hallow Hill, it's important to try to keep in mind what these images actually are, rather than allowing unexamined assumptions about their nature to take root. For all that their provenance is different, the sledging children and the skeletons have become inseparably conjoined. They've coalesced into one of the lenses in the compound eye through which my view of this place is mediated.

* * *

The second image is one I've transposed from elsewhere. Unlike the sledging children—and the skeletons—it's drawn from something that has no immediate connection with Hallow Hill and would never be found there. Yet despite its alien imported nature, it's become instrumental in how my view of this place is calibrated and framed.

Picture a yellowed grass stem growing in sandy ground near the sea. It's golden, dried out, holding the ripe grains of a seed head bleached almost white by the sun. About midway between the seed head and the ground, the narrow stem has a tiny swelling invisibly stitched to it, a pouch that's as long as the first joint of my little finger but only half as wide. It looks as if it were made out of waxed parchment; it's papery but tough, thickened yet translucent. It's almost as if the grass stem's single vein had grown varicose and bulged out to make this tiny pocket. It's affixed so beautifully it's hard to see a join; it almost seems like a natural part of the stem. Delicately engineered so that it's well within the grass's carrying capacity, it doesn't bend or break the stem. The pouch is empty, deflated. Closer examination reveals that it's been torn open. It has the air of a broken eggshell abandoned in a bird's nest, its contents gone. Although it's empty, the absence encircled by its structure suggests a recent presence.

When I was growing up in Ireland, my family visited Murlough Sand Dunes every summer. It's a stretch of undulating sandy ground laced with marram grass and wildflowers that runs down to the sea between Dundrum and Newcastle on the north-east coast of County Down. These little parchment pouches clung to many of the grass stems there. They are empty pupa cases, the remnant of the chrysalises of six-spot burnets, which we often saw flying in the unmistakable livery of iridescent red and black that characterizes this striking daytime-flying moth.

Just as my image of the sledging children is an incomplete mosaic put together from many sources, rather than a facsimile drawn with point-by-point exactitude from specific scenes, so with the pupa cases. To describe them as an *image* is misleadingly simplistic. That suggests something straightforwardly pictorial. It gives them a singularity and clarity that doesn't correspond to the way my mind draws them out of memory and attaches them, emblem-like, to the new setting of Hallow Hill. My image of them is as much a thing of textures, tempos, moods as it is a set of visual markers. Implicit in it is the whispering rattle of blown sand grains peppering the empty pupa cases, the parchment feel of them between the fingers, the smell of seaweed, the seemingly boundless duration of a childhood summer, the taste of salt on skin after swimming in the sea. The burnet pupae on the grass stems are held in a complex cocktail of sensations rather than being a purely visual and easily delineated thing. They're linked to, part of, a whole network of memories. But integral to this second image—which may be as much an idea, or a symbol, or the braided interplay of memory and imagination—is a sense of absent presence, of something gone, something vacated.

* * *

These, then, are the two images that, for me, have become so closely bound to Hallow Hill that whenever I think about the place or visit it, they are there, somewhere in mind, governing my outlook. Children sledging on snow laced with skeletons, and emptied six-spot burnet chrysalises may seem a curious choice of framing for what is quite an ordinary scene: a grassy rise of land with a scattering of trees that runs down to a stream crossed by a little metal footbridge. There's a narrow graveled path along one side of the hill. The place is frequented by walkers, often with dogs, and sometimes by runners. It offers a little oasis for birds and, every summer, wildflowers. But just to list these bare components of the place, what's immediately apparent about it, however much they may appear to constitute its reality, would be to offer so diluted a version of how it strikes me that it would incline more to deception than to documentary. To convey something of the flavor of my sense of Hallow Hill, it's necessary to foreground it with these two images that do so much to mold my understanding of this place.

The two images described, the power of their impact noted, let me explain the provenance of the skeletons. This will also make clear why empty burnet pupa cases became as tightly attached to my view of Hallow Hill as they were to their golden grass stems in those vanished childhood summers at Murlough Sand Dunes.

* * *

Hallow Hill is in present-day St Andrews, Scotland's ancient ecclesiastical capital but more famous now as the home of golf. There are no skeletons on the hill today—unless the archaeologists missed some. But go back far enough in time and the ground was thickly seeded with them. There are thought to have been around five hundred burials here, most dating from the seventh century. The graves were stone-lined and lidded with sandstone slabs brought from the coast a mile or two away, a style of grave known as a "long-cist" that was characteristic of the Picts, a people who inhabited Scotland at this time. They were direct descendants of the country's indigenous Iron Age population. In a rough timeline of human occupancy of Scotland, stretching from the Mesolithic (c. 8000 BC) to the present day, the Pictish period (sometimes dubbed "Early Historic") emerges around 500 AD and gradually fades into the Medieval period about four centuries later.

Uncertainty and conjecture surrounds the issue of who exactly the Picts were and what sort of a culture they created. Even the name by which we know them is not the name by which they knew themselves. If they had such a name it's lost to us. *Pict* is thought to derive from the Latin, *Pictii*, or painted. This is a likely reference to what the Roman invaders of Britain viewed as an outlandish practice of the aboriginals—namely, painting or tattooing themselves. The Irish name for them is *Cruithni*, meaning "people of the designs," though whether this referred to body art or the striking patterns they carved on stones is uncertain.

No Pictish writing survives. Our only written sources are in documents about them, written by those who viewed them as enemies or barbarians, which is hardly the best stance from which to derive accurate knowledge. The most striking material remnant of their culture, graves apart, takes the form of large stones carved with intriguing swirling symbols whose meaning no one has yet convincingly deciphered. It's thought that the Picts spoke a form of Celtic language, perhaps similar to that found in Cornwall, Wales, and Brittany. It's clear they didn't speak Gaelic. When Columba (c. 521–597), the famous Irish missionary saint, took the Christian message into the territory of the Picts, he needed interpreters to translate what he said into the local tongue. Their territory covered an impressive area of what is now Scotland, bounded in the south by the Forth and stretching north as far as Shetland and west to Skye. Yet despite the geographical extent of Pictland, and the ancientness of this people, the Picts disappeared. Their culture was absorbed into—swamped by—the emergent kingdom of the Scots.

The traces of the Picts that remain today seem fugitive, spectral, often mysterious. About twenty miles from St. Andrews, just outside the village of East Wemyss, there are caves that have been in human use for thousands of years. They contain carvings from Mesolithic right up to modern times, but by far the most striking and numerous of these carvings are Pictish in origin, dating from around 300–850 AD. There are abstract symbols, human figures, and beautifully realized animal studies. The people who drew them would certainly have known Hallow Hill; perhaps some of the artists were buried there. Several of the caves have been left open and are entirely unprotected, despite their archaeological significance. The cave walls are scrawled with contemporary graffiti. Empty bottles and beer cans litter the ground. In one cave there are the remains of a recent campfire. It seems somehow appropriate, if also lamentable, that a people who vanished from history, their identity melded into the surrounding milieu, their beliefs engulfed by Christianity, should have their remnant symbols at East Wemyss left vulnerable to the casual overlays of modernity.

* * *

Hallow Hill was an important Pictish cemetery. A small excavation was carried out there in 1861 by Charles Howie, who two years previously had discovered a Bronze Age cremation site at a nearby location. (Most of the twenty cinerary urns he discovered there are now in St. Andrews Museum.) Attracted by what was then named Halyhill—having previously been known as Alhallowhill, Hallahill, and Hallhallowhill—Howie thought this would be a good site to search for ancient graves. He uncovered five long-cists in the first instance. Three of the skulls recovered from them were presented to the St. Andrews Literary & Philosophical Society but have since been lost. Howie proceeded to unearth fifteen more long-cists. One of them contained Roman objects beside the remains of a child. Like the skulls, these objects too are now lost, although descriptions of them survive.

For the next century, Hallow Hill (as its name became and stayed after Howie's excavations) was in use as farmland. But at the beginning of the 1970s, in response to St Andrews' growing population, a development was proposed for residential housing on the hill. Public objection was so great that the area earmarked for development was significantly reduced in size and some of Hallow Hill became the public park that it remains today. But the rest, including part of the summit, was turned over to new housing. In the course of the building work an unknown number of cists were destroyed. Finally, alerted by the owner of one of the new houses to the presence of human bones in his garden, it was decided to organize a large-scale archaeological excavation of what remained of the site. This ran from 1975–1977 under the direction of Edwina Proudfoot. She and her team found 150 surviving cists, from an estimated total of five hundred.

The long-cists on Hallow Hill lay undisturbed for more than a thousand years. It's the knowledge of that long tenancy that makes me think of children sledging on snow that's underlain by bones, as it must actually have been for generations of the children who have sledged here. Seven cists have been left open to view. Six are adult-sized, though their occupants must have been of modest stature; the other one is obviously scaled to hold an infant. The sandstone slabs that would have sealed them have been removed and the contents are gone. Like the bones from all the excavated cists, they've been taken into museum storage. All that's left are seven shallow stone-walled indentations in a dip of ground at the top of the hill. Beside them there's an information board headed "Hallow Hill Pictish Cemetery." It gives some details about the site and its excavation, together with an artist's impression of what the area might have looked like fourteen centuries ago.

* * *

Any place is ancient simply by virtue of being part of Planet Earth. Scrape away whatever meets the eye, the immediacies of the familiar scene, any contemporary structures we've built on it, get down to the bedrock, and a scale of time that dwarfs our usual measures soon becomes apparent. There are eons woven into the plainest stones beneath our feet, a point made beautifully by Jan Zalasiewicz in his remarkable book *The Planet in a Pebble* (2010). Taking a pebble from a beach, Zalasiewicz shows that once we learn to decipher its cargo, the pebble, as his title suggests, contains no less than the story of the planet. His book is a masterclass in how extraordinary the ordinary things around us are.

If they had sensation, the stones on Hallow Hill would have felt the reverberation of the tread that long extinct life-forms once laid upon the ground above them. The stones that are threaded through the earth of this Pictish cemetery are mute witnesses not just to how a vanished people disposed of their dead fourteen centuries ago but to the millions of years that preceded human existence. And they will remain here long after all of us have gone. It's easy to imagine a place only within the ambit of our use for it, so that Hallow Hill appears simply as a quiet place to walk or run or exercise a dog, a patch of common green surrounded by private housing that allows access to a riverside path and a shortcut into town. But this place, like every place, has a history that's on a scale that makes all our comings and goings seem miniature, recent, and short-lived. It's hard to get a proper grasp of its ancientness. Even thinking back to when it was being seeded with long-cists only encompasses a tiny fraction of its age. Hallow Hill long predated them; human agency represents only the tiniest fraction of what has happened here.

* * *

The seven visible cists, and the information board about the Pictish cemetery that they're part of, will clearly have a profound impact on the way in which people see this place, myself included. If these cists had been covered over again post-excavation—like the scores of others that surround them and now lie unseen, buried again beneath the earth and grass—and if no information board had been erected, it's unlikely I would have seen Hallow Hill as anything more than the modest rise of land that meets the eye. The sledging children in their bright apparel that I associate so strongly with this place would have been playing on ordinary, bone-free snow. The image of the empty moth pupae would never have occurred to me. It was drawn from memory and battened onto Hallow Hill only because of the empty cists. However different these stone chambers might seem to the papery husks of the burnet chrysalises, it was the vacated nature of both that called up this linkage and made it seem an apt, even necessary association. Shorn of any knowledge of its past, Hallow Hill would have struck a quite different resonance. I'd have seen it, understood it according to a different set of images, and these might have had almost no resemblance to the ones that I'm describing here.

I'm reminded of something John Berger says about how strongly words can influence how we see things. On one page of Berger's book *Ways of Seeing* (1972), Van Gogh's painting *Wheatfield with Crows* is reproduced with only the painting's title and the artist's name and dates written beside it (and of course, name and date will themselves already exert an influence). On the next page the same painting is shown—but this time with the caption: "This is the last picture that Van Gogh painted before he killed himself." Berger comments: "It is hard to define exactly how the words have changed the image but undoubtedly they have." Likewise with the information board at Hallow Hill. I don't think I could describe how I saw the place before and after reading it, or list the differences between those two seeings one by one. But looking at the board brought a significant change to my reading of the hill. It's as if its words leant their weight against the raw visual lineaments and bent them into different shapes, tuned them to a different key.

* * *

I began this exploration of the meaning of a place by saying that two images have become so closely bound to Hallow Hill that it requires a special effort for me to see past them to the reality of the place itself. But already in that statement there's a nub of complications. How do images become bound to a place? How do they affect our perception of it? What are *images* in any case, and is it possible to see past them? I've become suspicious of the concept of "the reality of the place itself" and increasingly doubt whether it's possible to reach it. Thinking in terms of seeing past images to a reality beyond them seems to downgrade the former to something illusory and privilege the latter with some kind of singular correctness. It's easy to slip into assuming that images are unreal, secondary, merely imagined—that they're removed from "the place itself" and act only to obscure the truth of the matter from us.

But the more I think about it, the more I'm unsure about the way in which a place lays its nature upon us, or what that nature is, or whether we're equipped to grasp more than a fraction of it. And if we each do that grasping in our own particular way, Hallow Hill—like anywhere—will strike different individuals very differently, we will all interpose our own particular images and memories and associations, coloring the lenses of perception. How then could we ever presume to know who has grasped "the reality of the place itself"? Perhaps the complete inventory of different people's views of it over time would better approach an apprehension of what's there than any single point of view, however much that point of view may lay claim to being rooted in plain facts, unadorned by individual imaginings. Is it possible that our favored model of accuracy—taking it to be a kind of uncompromising solitaire, adamantine in the precision with which each facet of its certainty is cut—may be misleading and that something cloudier, softer, more malleable and plural better contours the way things are? Perhaps we each contribute to "the reality of a place" rather than its being a single unchanging stratum to be discovered underlying all our individual perceptions.

Maybe answers to some of these interlocking questions—or at least the beginning of answers—will suggest themselves along the way. But rather than trying to resolve them directly, I want simply to acknowledge their existence and concentrate on what's personal and particular—the way Hallow Hill appears to me and how I've come to understand its nature over a period of years. I make no pretense to reveal "the reality of the place itself." My concern is simply to lay down on the page the way this place strikes me. The emphasis on the single thread of one person's perception will, I hope, cast more light on the fabric of the place than a depersonalized description would do. Such a depersonalized description might claim universal validity because it privileges abstraction over specificity and tries to purge the individual from its outlook. The objectivity such an approach supposedly offers may be alluring, but it seems ill-suited to showing with any subtlety the actual textures that are woven when place and person interact.

* * *

Sometimes when I walk there now, it seems as if the hill is hollow. I picture it as a giant chrysalis, honeycombed with individual cells, each one emptied of its occupant. Only the parchment casing is left to ring drum-like under my tread, my steps sounding out a haunting tattoo of emptiness. This sense of absence, imagining that the hill is no more than a kind of husk, that its grassy slope is just a thin integument stretched over empty chambers, clearly doesn't tally with the actual nature of the place. The ground here is as solid as it is elsewhere. From a commonsense perspective, my imaginings of hollowness are fanciful. Whatever credibility they can claim is rooted not in the solid substance of the ground as it lies reliably supportive underfoot, but in what's suggested by the empty cists left open on display and the knowledge that all of the graves in this ancient necropolis have been systematically emptied.

As well as drawing a measure of metaphorical validity from the emptied cists, the sense of hollowness that attends this place is also strengthened by something more wide-ranging: the knowledge that Hallow Hill represents not just the vanishing of a few hundred skeletons but of an entire people. The Picts who filled this place with their dead fourteen hundred years ago disappear from the historical record in the ninth century—precisely when Hallow Hill fell into disuse and was abandoned. The Picts' disappearance didn't come about with the dramatic abruptness of extermination or extinction. It was more a case of their gradual assimilation into the races and cultures that were flourishing around them. Nonetheless, for all that they blend into the emergent milieu rather than being violently excised from it, their disappearance adds piquancy to the sense of emptiness and loss that Hallow Hill engenders (a sense that summoned, and is fed by, my memory of the empty burnet chrysalises).

The abandonment of this cemetery is symbolic of cessation on a far larger scale than the discontinuance of burials at one local site; it's emblematic of the way in which the Picts were washed away by stronger currents in Scottish history. However much its immediate impact is simply one of unremarkable presence—a grassy open space, a gentle gradient running down to a stream, the feel of firm ground underfoot, the sound of running water, birdsong, leaves moving in the breeze—Hallow Hill for me is underlain by an almost tangible sense of absence. For all that their occupancy of this part of Scotland extended over centuries, the Picts were a passing feature of the landscape, not a permanent part of it. Their transience is a reminder of our own.

* * *

Looking around its present-day environs, I try to get a sense of the slow shift of centuries that has happened on Hallow Hill between the Pictish burials and now, between their time and mine. Over that small fraction of its history, what has been hosted on the stage this place provides? The pages of time's score that represent the centuries between the bodies being laid in the long cists and their excavation by archaeologists may seem to bear upon them only sparse notation, a few long, repetitive notes that issue in a kind of monotone, the low-pitched drone of mere continuance—more like a background hum than any tune that we can sing along with. But this would be to assume that the music of being plays no notes other than the melodies and discords of our presence. If we attune our imaginative ear more keenly, learn to listen beyond the trills and variations of our human noise, there are notes of orchestral complication sounding here. For vast spans of its history the harmonics of this place were set at pitches and timed to rhythms that we normally don't register.

Think of the deep liquid breathing sounded by the seepage of water, ton by ton, as it slowly sluiced through the earth. Within this gigantic inhalation and exhalation there's the harsher note of erosion, as particles held in the liquid embrace of droplets gently abrade whatever they flow past. Threaded through with sediment, it's as if the water bears within it invisible teeth that chew and grind the land, sculpting it into shape. Rain's metronome sets the beat. The annual carpeting with autumn's leaves feeds a gradual leeching of minerals into the earth. Snow adds its cold constriction, magnifying the pressure that's placed on these few acres with the weight of ten million snowflakes compacting on the earth. There's a millimetric shift and settling within the earth as seeds grow, roots stretch, bodies decompose, insects burrow.

Listen, and you can also hear the soulful chant of repeated nightfall as the dark embraces Hallow Hill at the end of every day. Alongside the sound of wind in trees there's the stealthy note of air passing through the muffling barbules of owls' feathers as they fly deadly through the dusk. The soft impact of a pounce as an owl falls upon a mouse sends a tiny shiver vibrating through a patch of earth, below which snowdrop bulbs are wakening to life. The talons' puncture adds its cadence to scores of moments through the centuries as generations of owls and mice collide in their ballet of predation and prey. Over fourteen centuries what weight of owl feathers, owl excrement, mouse bones would have accumulated on Hallow Hill?

A leaf falls, a feather floats gently to the ground, a twig drops from a bird's nest, dandelion seeds soundlessly pepper the grass: such little impacts have been a regular soft staccato keeping time to rhythms that long predate our advent. Has blood shed here—by owl or kestrel, fox or stoat—trickled redly to the ground and penetrated far enough to stain for a moment the white bones of the Picts laid out in their long cists? As the clustered corpses are dismantled by the processes of decay, as bacteria and insects orchestrate the changes we rely on, they add their own themes to the music playing here. Listen, and you can hear the tremor of a fox's stealthy tread, its nighttime hunting resulting in bones and fur and blood that add minutely to the substance of the hill. Listen, and you can also just make out the voices of the roots of grass and flowers and trees edging incrementally through the earth, their woody veins and capillaries suckling from there the substances they need. The weather conducts its movements year by year. Night follows day. Time passes, weaving its skein of events around Hallow Hill.

* * *

The seven cists left open to view each trace out narrow rectangular shapes, contoured to fit the dimensions of the bodies they once held. They range from infant to adult size. The excavation found a far higher proportion of children and infants among the dead than would be the case in a modern cemetery, a reminder of how much shorter an average lifespan was and how much more precarious life used to be. These seven cists lie in an untidy cluster in a shallow dip of land at the top of Hallow Hill, close to the garden of one of the houses whose building caused such archaeological havoc. The presence of the cists is explained by the information board that's been erected beside them. But for me these emptied sepulchers act not like real-life illustrations obedient to what's written on the board. Instead, they're like opaque mirrors that reflect back their own mute emptiness, announcing the fact that what they held is gone. Their nullity of reflection exerts a kind of magnetism, pulling me into a blankness that sparks an insistent curiosity about what they once contained.

Notwithstanding the actual shape and arrangement of the seven open cists you can see today, I often see the little dip of land they occupy as emblazoning the hill's summit with a flotilla of question marks. What were the names of the individuals who were laid here long ago? What ideas flickered through their consciousnesses? What were their hopes and dreams, their favorite foods? What paths did their lives follow? Had they visited the caves in East Wemyss, looked at the carvings there that we can still admire today? What were their last thoughts before they died? Did they believe that death was the end, or had the missionary efforts of St Columba instilled a hope of life to come? Who shed tears for them? Did the hands that buried them do so with anguish, or disgust, or fear, or simple workaday practicality? How did Hallow Hill appear to them and their friends and families; what images did the place spark in Pictish minds?

Many of these questions would find answers readily enough if we could travel back in time and just observe, if we could talk to the Picts in their own language, understand their words. But alongside the quotidian questions about the fine detail of their vanished lives, the seven open long-cists are loaded with a different category of question, a type whose posing makes me think that the opaque mirrors that they hold up to existence are like black holes. They swallow every possibility of answer. Like any grave, however recent or ancient, these ones can interrogate anyone who walks past them, make them wonder about how and when they'll meet their own quietus; what they believe about consciousness; if there's anything beyond our mortal end; whether our lives and deaths can claim any meaning beyond whatever can be gleaned from the repertoire of daily experience that's acted out in the span of days we occupy.

If you do a Google image search for "Hallow Hill St Andrews," one of the pictures that comes up features some girls in brightly colored jackets lying in the open cists. It's as if they're trying on a kind of Cinderella's shoe or playacting at a future state they know they'll occupy but that is, for the moment, far enough away to hold no terror. They look like tourists, perhaps visiting for the first time. I wonder how Hallow Hill appeared to them, what images they brought to it, what images they took away, how the place struck them compared to how it strikes me. And what would the Picts have thought of these young bodies light-heartedly japing death in the cists in which they once laid real corpses?

* * *

When they reported on their excavations of the long-cists, the archaeologists numbered them and described what each one contained. So I know that cist 26 (since covered over) held the skeleton of a female, aged between thirty-five and thirty-nine. Her bones were marked with evidence of leprosy, though whether this disease caused or only hastened her death is uncertain. Standing at the open cists, I sometimes wonder about this afflicted individual whose bones used to lie just a little distance away. All the building blocks of flesh and blood and breath that made her have long been tumbled from the intricate arrangements that built her unique personality; all the intimate combinations of organic parts and processes that interlocked to make her the person that she was have been separated, dissolved, destroyed. So is she, as appearances so strongly suggest, lost forever, utterly gone beyond any hope of retrieval? Or is it possible that some spark or soul or splinter—an essence of her—somewhere survives and carries with it, coded into some mysterious interstice of being that we've not yet discovered how to decipher, the precise gleam of intelligence that once twinkled in her eyes, the exact set of her shoulders expressing the pain and humiliation of the disease that disfigured her? As with all of us, the weather of her experience will have eroded the landscape of her person into a highly particular set of plains, gullies, gradients, and other features. Does anything of that topography survive, safely jettisoned into some unknown realm, or has it all vanished as completely as her breathing? Is there any trace left anywhere in the universe that would correspond to the "I" she thought of as herself? Is she still in existence somewhere, somehow? And if so, is she purged of the suffering she carried with her, or was it sutured to her so tightly, so much a part of who she was, that any preservation of some essential remnant must preserve it also? Or, far from any such incredible survival, has the individual in cist 26 been annihilated, rendered into the anonymous building blocks of matter, lost utterly and forever?

* * *

The archaeologists' numbering of the long-cists on Hallow Hill makes me think about numbering on a far wider scale. If every grave there's ever been was given a number, is it credible to suppose that of the billions there would be, every individual could have the fleeting uniqueness of who they were protected and preserved? According to Worldometers (www.worldometers.info/), a website that plots world population, when I was born I was the 76,136,299,830th representative of *Homo sapiens* to appear on

Earth. Is it possible that the thoughts that arced through all the brains of those who came before me, that will arc through all those who have and will come after me, all the feelings that have coursed through this enormous multitude of bodies, the catalogues of memories that all of us have garnered—could each single one be kept, distinct and individual and safe, forever?

Sometimes when I stand on Hallow Hill, I think of it as a microcosm of the world, the globe of Earth, like this small acre, seeded with the dead and walked on by the living, a catafalque spinning honeycombed in space, bearing countless bones within it, and all of us who live upon its surface, like my image of the sledging children, stepping our way over ground that's thickly threaded with the skeletons of those who came before us. And in the anonymity of gigantic numbers—the fact that our planet is 4600 million years old, an infinitesimal part of a universe that came into being over 13 billion years ago and that contains hundreds of billions of galaxies; the fact that each one of us consists of innumerable cells, innumerable atoms; the fact that there are seven billion of us now—it seems inconceivable that nothing will be lost, that all of humanity's teeming plethora of complex selves will somehow trump time and death and history and survive, intact, complete, whatever we hold most precious preserved.

The woman in cist 26 has gone; there is no way that I could ever meet her, smile and talk, reach out my hand to touch her, ask her name. She and her people have disappeared from history, as I will, as we all will. I wish the image of the burnet pupae suggested resurrection, eternal life, but I fear it points only to the lifecycle that we're part of. The seven empty cists on Hallow Hill don't indicate any escape or miraculous transformation. They are, rather, potently suggestive of our humanness—the fragile continuance of life and our sadness when it ends. The individuals who bear that life across the generations, through the centuries, for whatever purpose, perish; none of us is made for permanence.

* * *

Sometimes now I go to the exact spot on Hallow Hill where I know that under the grass and earth beneath my feet cist 54 is buried. There's nothing to show where it is. I rely on the archaeological maps to find my way to its location. This was an unusual two-tiered grave that the archaeologists thought might be particularly important, perhaps marking the first interment, a kind of center point or pivot around which the graveyard grew. Nothing remained in the upper tier, but in the lower one the bones of a child were discovered, together with a collection of artifacts. These are described in the published records as being "found close together, lying across the pelvis and left thigh of the child in a manner suggestive of a purse or drawstring bag or pouch."

Standing there, I try to imagine the scene that was played out so long ago in human terms, so recently when measured against the chronology of stone. Of course it's impossible to retrieve the actual texture of the moment, to unearth the exact detail of what happened. There is much we can never know, much that is mere supposition. Who was the child? What caused so early a death? Did he or she have siblings who flourished, who may even have left a trace in a long line of descendants stretching from their time into mine.

What's certain is that a child of five or six years old was buried here at this precise spot where I'm standing, the body laid to rest in a stone-lined grave not far beneath the grass whose stems, 1400 years later, are temporarily flattened by my weight. To express their love and loss, someone, most likely parents, collected an assemblage of little objects to bury with their child. These were surely invisibly imbued with personal meaning and meant to stand proxy for a hand held tightly, a hug, a farewell kiss upon the brow. The objects lay undisturbed for centuries. There are some childish treasures, no doubt favorite things (pebbles, a piece of quartz crystal, some cow's teeth), and items of adult value (a ring, a brooch, and a seal box).

Echoing the finds made at the child's grave excavated by Charles Howie in 1861, the three manufactured items in cist 54 were of Roman origin and date from the first to third centuries AD. This means they were already four or five hundred years old by the time they were buried on Hallow Hill. How they came into the Picts' possession is unknown. Perhaps a Roman galley once called in for provisioning at St Andrews or another nearby port and the seal box and other items were traded. Perhaps they were plunder from piracy.

The Roman occupation of Britain lasted for close to four hundred years, from 43–410 AD. But for the most part the northernmost frontier was marked by Hadrian's Wall, and Roman incursions into Scotland were few and of relatively short duration. We don't know how Romans and Picts interacted in the periods when both had a presence in Scotland. Maybe the artifacts originated from the large military camp at Carpow in nearby Perthshire.

Maybe they were part of a bride price or dowry. They could have been stolen, given, sold, or part of a ransom. Whatever their provenance, to use as grave goods what must surely have been valuable heirlooms suggests both wealth and the depth of sorrow that this child's death occasioned.

* * *

Because it is so well preserved and so intrinsically appealing, and because it lay buried on a child's lap for fourteen centuries, the seal box is a particularly potent object for me—so much so that it's become a kind of triangulation point for Hallow Hill, pulling it into focus and gently nudging my thoughts and feelings into their particular alignments. The seal box almost acts like a compass, though one that doesn't point unerringly to the True North of what happened. Instead it swivels uncertainly between that and my reading of the evidence; it provides a hinge, opening a tiny portal into the history I imagine happening in this place.

A description of its appearance doesn't remotely catch this object's gravity. The seal box is like a chasm, a pothole in time, a crevasse in the ordinary passage of the days, disrupting their routine chronology with another sense of duration. I miss my footing at its brink, stumble, and am drawn into other times, other places, into other lives and fates.

How it meets the eye is pleasing, but the voltage that the seal box carries is invisible. Made of bronze and the appealingly named *millefiori* (thousand flowers), a technique of using colored glass, this beautifully worked artifact would once have held a seal used to imprint the owner's mark on wax. Only 30 mm in diameter and 8 mm in depth, this little round container fits easily in the palm. When it was retrieved from the child's grave on Hallow Hill it was empty, a fact revealed by X-ray since the box is too fragile to risk forcing open, the iron pin securing the hinged lid fused with rust. I sometimes think of how astounded the Roman craftsman who made it would have been—likewise all its owners—if they were able to glimpse their seal box's story. Its journey through space is astonishing enough, ending up on the very periphery of Roman influence, on or beyond the outermost edge of what its makers and owners would have regarded as civilization. But its journey through time is even more incredible. Buried on a Scottish hillside several centuries after it was made, lying there for more than a thousand years as life unfolded in all its intricate complexity above it, then found, cleaned, and studied before being catalogued and hoarded within a museum's cache of treasures, where the bright colors of the *millefiori* (blue, yellow, red, white) can still delight the eye in the twenty-first century. They are as vivid today as when they were seen through the tear-stained eyes of those who mourned the child and put this token in its grave.

For me, the voltage the seal box carries, the electricity that flows through it, the charge of significance it holds, only become properly apparent when I think of it not in terms of sight but of touch. I like to picture the moment when, after lying cold in the earth for centuries, the seal box was once more warmed by a human hand. It's an item that after its manufacture would have been kept about the person, taking on the body heat of whoever owned it. Thinking of its last blood temperature moment, when it was placed by a living hand into the pouch tied around the dead child's waist, and its being warmed again by the archaeologist who found it, the seal box takes on the guise of a stitch closing the wound of time, bringing together—despite the gulf of years that separate them—the person who last held it in the seventh century and the person who first held it again the twentieth. It seems like a kind of suture stitched across a gash of centuries so that time's flow is momentarily staunched, frozen, and we can tentatively walk across the ice of healing that it offers.

In one sense I know that this is fanciful. I'm not sure of the identity of the person who dug it up, let alone that of the person who buried it. They are both strangers to me. But it is an indubitable fact, diamond hard in the durability of its certainty, that there was a last person to hold it, to warm it in their hand in the seventh century, and a first person to do so in the twentieth. Though it bears upon it nothing perceptible that gives testimony to either of these (or any other) holdings, I'm as sure of both as I'm sure that this little object is a solid not a liquid. So when it lies cupped in my own palm and my blood slowly warms it again, I feel a fleeting sense of fugitive connection, even though I know the narrative nerve that links everyone who's ever touched it can't be reconstructed or resuscitated beyond conjecture, and that any imagined impulse coursing through it is no more than that—imagined.

* * *

In order to hold the seal box, I had to make special arrangements. It's kept in a secure, low-humidity store and is not on public display. But museum staff were happy enough, when I explained my interest, to withdraw it temporarily from this protective environment and let me examine it. In the clinical surroundings of a museum workroom, the curator and I handled it as delicately as if it were a rare bird's egg. It's small enough to be one, though the shape is wrong. Circular rather than oval and instead of the round fullness traced out by an eggshell's curve, the base of the seal box is flat. It sits on the bench without rolling. The top likewise lacks any swelling out into an egg's ripe curve. But it is rich in a sense of what can hatch from it, and the decorative glass with which it's inlaid makes it as appealing as the colored patterns on any bird's egg. I asked some questions and examined the seal box closely, admiring the *millefiori* work and the skill with which the glass has been set into the metal. It's amazingly well preserved for something that lay buried in the earth for so long. But alongside this rational examination—and out of place, I know, in a museum context—I also felt a kind of shamanic current emanating from this little archaeological find.

Was it superstition, or sentiment, or a desire to close some intangible circuit, or to symbolically return an egg to the nest it had been raided from that led me back to Hallow Hill straight after my museum visit? I made my way to where cist 54 is situated and placed my hand on the grass above it, as if in benediction. Three feet below my reach was the rock-lined earth cradle that had held the child's body. The seal box and the other tokens and treasures that were put in the drawstring purse tied around the little waist lay here for fourteen centuries. Now the bones are gone, bagged and boxed and labeled in a museum store, along with all the other skeletons from Hallow Hill. The drawstring purse is long decayed and its trove of objects taken, catalogued, and cached. My hand has nothing in it. But even if somehow it held the seal box, I know I could not restore it. The nest is empty. The birds have flown. Time has moved on.

* * *

It's unlikely I'd ever have discovered Hallow Hill if it hadn't been for the fact that when I moved to St Andrews in 2010 the house I bought there just happened to be near it, in fact on the road whose route an ancient cobbled road made by the Picts once followed to the coast. It's strange to think that fourteen centuries ago carts laden with sandstone slabs to roof the long-cists would have passed close by what's now my garden, the people with them speaking a language I wouldn't understand, looking out on a world I'd only recognize in part. They would have had viewpoints that, if I could share them, I suspect I'd find an unnerving mix of alien and familiar. The fact that Hallow Hill was there, right on my doorstep, wasn't something I realized to begin with; I discovered it by chance. But now I know it's there and what it represents, it's become a place I walk to often. If the distance were not so slight, I'd be tempted to say that I make regular pilgrimages to it. For there's something about the place, or how I see it, that suggests my visits are prompted by more than a desire for fresh air and exercise. If I simply want to walk, St Andrews is full of more appealing routes and destinations than the muddy paths that take me to this modest little hillock.

My ordinary vision, what meets the eye any day I go there, only registers a quotidian scene of dog walkers, children, birds, grass, and trees. But I see Hallow Hill quite differently from anything suggested by them. Or do I mean I *think* of it, or *imagine* it, quite differently? It's hard to know the best locution to describe the operation of that inner gaze that the mind's eye lays on the purely ocular and that does so much to determine how a place lays its presence on the psyche. Whatever name is given, it acts like a secret catalyst on plain seeing, resulting in outlooks that could never be predicted merely by describing the catalogue of shapes, colors, textures, and movements that fall immediately upon the eye. Every present-day dog walker and runner, like every Pict laid to rest here, will have their own store of images, associations, information, memories and experience out of which the unique torque and cut and tincture of their outlook will be fashioned. But however carefully I might attempt to make word-cists to hold them, I know that none of these individual intimacies of outlook can be preserved for long.

* * *

History is as easily sloughed off the things that bear witness to its passing as the scales rub off a butterfly's wings. Even those objects that are dramatically entangled with what happened tend to reach us purged of any trace of the specifics of their involvement. So, for example, if we hold a World War I bayonet in our hands, we are helpless to establish beyond the uncertainty of reasonable conjecture the precise part it played in that terrible conflict. Unless something comes to us already documented, we cannot directly sense the story it is part of. But I sometimes wonder if what happens really does evaporate from things as quickly and completely as it seems to. Perhaps things have inscribed on their deep structure, at an atomic level, invisibly tattooed into the protons and electrons and nuclei that constitute their fundamental core, an indelible record of the trajectories they have followed through time and space, and their involvement, if any, with our human stories. Maybe we have yet to learn how to access and read these automatic logbooks that keep meticulous account of all that passes, and that when we do the Braille of the world's substance will sing and speak and howl as we brush our questing fingers over it, everything made fluent to their touch.

Sometimes I dream of being given another sense, one that is as sensitive to the stories that are invisibly carved into things as the eyes are sensitive to light, so that I could tell from the touch of anything on my flesh the history it had followed prior to that moment of revelatory contact. Such a sense could seek out the script that's written in the interstices of the seal box's deep structure, like strands of DNA carrying the genes of its existence, or a manifest recording all the occurrences that have happened, what time's passing has brushed against it. It could touch the bones from cist 26 and cist 54 and render them into flutes that would play out the music of that nameless woman and child.

But such an extravagant ability to sense the nature of things would place so great a burden of information on the psyche that it might fracture and perish beneath the weight. Fascinating though it would be to hold the seal box in my hand and listen to its voice, hear a complete account of the odyssey it has taken, the nerves of narrative that this would awaken would soon ignite into an unmanageable conflagration. The story of the box itself, from manufacture to burial and retrieval, would be complex enough, with every hand that ever touched it offering a route to follow into other lives and places, each replete with their own dense nexus of connections. But the raw materials with which it's made—the copper and tin and iron and glass—would all have within them a cacophony of information.

This imagined sixth sense would be a two-edged thing indeed. Its blade might cut through the dumbness of things and afford us wonderful insights, but how would we staunch the flow of what would be unleashed from its incisions? And if, like our other senses, this one was at its most intense when making love, would we really welcome the depth of knowledge given and received? Would it heighten or hamper ecstasy to see a beloved's history laid out in all its naked abundance, stretching back through successive generations to the moment life began (and to have our own time lines read by our partners in return)? Or what if our fingers happened to brush against a fossil that had been formed four hundred million years ago? The terabytes of data that would flood out from it would surely carry a voltage as likely to annihilate as to delight or enlighten. Perhaps it's just as well that we can see into the history of things only as far as the limits of our information and imagination. Were history directly readable by touch it would soon overwhelm the present.

* * *

Sometimes I think of the leprosy-afflicted woman whose body was placed in cist 26. Did she know the child buried in cist 54? Were they members of the same family, or neighbors, or were they strangers despite the small-scale communities in which the Picts lived? Of course, though they're laid to rest only a stone's throw apart, they may have lived at different times. Not all the skeletons have been dated, but it's clear that Hallow Hill was in use for several generations. The patterns of kin and friendship that may link those buried here are among the many things it's hard to reconstruct, at least with our current techniques for peering into the past and reading its secrets. Perhaps in another 1400 years the bones stored in the museum vaults will be subjected to new techniques of inquiry that will yield such information.

I wonder how similar the outlook of the woman in cist 26 would have been to mine. Apart from obvious differences dictated by language, gender, point in history, might some things have seemed more or less the same despite the gulfs between us? Pollen analysis shows, for example, that many of the plant species that meet contemporary eyes around Hallow Hill would have met her eyes too 1400 years ago. Cold and clouds and leaves and rain and sunshine warm upon the skin surely form a kind of common vocabulary of experience that both of us would have learned, however differently we might name its constituents. I may not know her word for the tree we now call "alder," or how she would have expressed her pleasure at a fine spring day, but the elements behind such things would be more likely to act as a link and bond and common ground between us than as a barrier. How we feel cold and love and pain, the pleasure of good food and company, the way fear can ambush us in the dark—such things would surely fall upon us without significant differences.

But that obvious insoluble puzzle of the everyday remains: how does another person see the world? It is given an added savor of impossibility when so much time separates two individuals. A seventh century Pictish mindset would have been founded on such a different knowledge base to ours that it's possible everything that percolated through it would be so radically different that we'd find it hard to recognize any of the familiar handholds by which we take cognizance of our situation. Think of how cist 26 would have understood the leprosy that afflicted her, what she'd have taken for cause and cure; think of her grasp of the size and shape of planet Earth; think of how little knowledge she'd have had to hand about the origin and development of life. She would not have known Africa or Asia or Australia, let alone the solar system. She was innocent of electricity, TV, computers, atom bombs, genocide, and global warming. Who knows what ideas would have been fomented by the Christian teaching newly laid on traditional beliefs? Coded into her network of perception would have been the Pictish words for *stream* and *hill*, for *snow* and *moth*, for *love* and *loss*—a whole catechism of categories in which the world was cupped and held, each carrying its own cargoes of association. Whatever web of perception netted her view of things, pulled in her harvest of impressions, it could as easily have been profoundly different from mine as similar, however much its threads ran over common territory. And of course she'd have known Hallow Hill as a burial ground, with all the sorrow that entails, not as a recreational space that happens also to possess an interesting archaeological dimension. The place would have appeared through a radically different set of associations.

* * *

If I kneel down and reach out my hand, I can touch the stones on the open cists at the summit of Hallow Hill, the stones placed there by Pictish hands fourteen centuries before I came to walk here. My fingers rest on the cold surface, momentarily warming it, as it would have been flesh-warmed by whoever made these stone chrysalises. But despite our proximity in space, the fact that I can occupy exactly the same coordinates as the ones those ancient grave makers must have occupied, the distance in time between us mocks any sense of closeness, however much I might feel and desire it. Yet despite the icy centuries freezing out their isolating expanse between us, despite the fact that we leave so little trace of our lives, it sometimes feels as if there are some fugitive traces in this place of those who were associated with it for so long. It's thought some local places still retain the ghost of Pictish culture in their names. Those starting with *Pit*, for example, are said to retain an element of this vanished people's vanished language. So Pitscottie, Pittenweem, Pitsligo, Pitlochry stand testament to territory the Picts once occupied. (It's tentatively suggested that *pit* may have meant a share or piece of land.) Perhaps when the wind blows from a certain direction and at a certain speed and hits Hallow Hill at a particular angle, the noises that it kindles contain ghosts of the words that were spoken here long ago, husks of sound that once carried meaning.

Given the extinction of which this place is so strongly suggestive, it's no wonder that it should act as a memento mori. In writing about it here I'm following what is, I suppose, a natural response to the imminence and certainty of death and dissolution—a weaving of words to place on the sharp blade of finitude in the hope of scabbarding it with some sense of sense, blunting the edge of nothingness with hints of meaning that it might not cut. But do the lifelines that language seems to offer really name anything beyond the intricately coiled knots of our own desires and utterances?

The more I reflect about the nature of Hallow Hill and how I perceive it, the more weight I'm inclined to give to a whole array of idiosyncratic coordinates by means of which we mark on our individual navigation charts the contour lines of feelings, interconnections, objects, and events that we associate with a place. I know my view of Hallow Hill has changed quite markedly from the first time I visited it. Initially, it was just part of a walk, one of the town's green spaces. I hadn't known about the Picts. I'd not noticed the cists left open at the summit or the information board beside them. Once I did, the whole ambience of the place shifted, making me wonder to what extent a place changes when our image of it changes. And I wonder, too, about whether this cemetery should have been excavated, whether it's right to remove the human remains that lay here, whether the child's bones in cist 54 should have been separated from the treasures laid beside them. Has time interposed enough years of buffering to overrule considerations that would make us stay our hand and shy away from visiting such despoliation on more recent burials? Has the sorrow evaporated so completely from the seal box that it's acceptable just to treat it as a find—and inter it in the bland bureaucratic burial of a museum's holdings, something to be signed in and out and examined with curiosity?

* * *

I began this meditation on Hallow Hill with the two things that have come to frame it for me: children sledging on bone-threaded snow, and the empty cases of burnet moth chrysalises. I've also tried to explain how the seal box has come to act as a kind of triangulation point or compass, a point of reference I keep touching. I don't want to end with a conclusion. Conclusions sit smugly after the ritual of considering arguments for and against has been performed, their presence suggesting something cut and dried and final, something arrived at via processes that are linear, logical, well structured. Instead, I want to give the last word to two gestures that I find almost consoling. They bring a sense of humaneness, humanity—perhaps even hope—into a setting that often seems brutal in the absence that it brokers, bleak in its fealty to the unbending processes of time that govern it, the iron fist of mortality within every velvet glove with which we try to soften it.

The first gesture was made by the Picts themselves. In choosing a sandstone slab to be part of the roofing capstone of one of the long-cists (the archaeologists numbered it 69), it looks as if the stone was deliberately selected because it bore on it the imprint of a fossilized plant. Of course, it would have been the immediate decorative potential lent to the slab by this eons-old tracery of leaf and stem, rather than any knowledge of what it was, that led to its being chosen. I find it oddly reassuring to think of a human body laid to rest in a stone capsule that's embossed with a naturally occurring emblem of this kind, even if the Picts were innocent of what it betokened. This stone bears witness to an ancientness that makes the distance between me and them seem negligible, and that speaks of the processes of life and death happening repeatedly, predictably, unwaveringly over so many millions of millennia that it instills them with a weight and momentum of inevitability that offer solace in the face of the tragedy of individual extinction.

The second gesture is one made by people today. Someone has planted primroses in some of the opened cists. Their blooms appear each spring and last for months. And every now and then posies of wildflowers, or—more rarely—bought cut flowers, are left. Sometimes the cut flowers coincide with the scattering of human ashes. I warm to such flower planting, flower leaving, and the use of Hallow Hill as a place to lay the remnants of our modern dead. I know how vulnerable such things are to any assessment of their logic. Who is being remembered, if remembrance this is? Is it a gesture of sorrow, solidarity, or mere sentimentality? Why mark this patch of earth rather than some other with the gift of flowers? And why choose these ancient graves as the sepulcher for the contemporary remains from cremation? What do the people who do this hope to achieve or express by their action?

No one can claim any real connection with the cluster of bodies once entombed here, which in any case are gone, transformed from the husks of individuals into archaeological specimens held in the clinical environs of a museum storeroom. No one knows the names of the Picts who were buried on Hallow Hill. No one knows what they dreamt of, what they hoped for. There is nothing of these people left. Yet to honor the unknown dead like this, to lay the ashes of our own dead among the empty stone pupae on Hallow Hill is to make a gesture that's rich in respect and remembrance—even reverence—and that seems gravid with a sense of significance beyond the ordinary, even if the symbolism it draws on is hard to fathom, harder to justify. In the wordless eloquence of choosing a decorative rock as coffin lid and in planting or leaving flowers on the graves of ancient strangers, and scattering our own ashes here, is there perhaps a vein of meaning we might tap, a sense of connection with something that glimmers, pale as a primrose, with possibilities beyond the obvious?

The empty chrysalises of six-spot burnets are a potent memory from my childhood visits to Murlough Sand Dunes. I also remember what we took to be their equally eye-catching caterpillars, brightly striped in black and yellow. Sometimes there were scores of these fat tiger grubs feeding on the yellow-bloomed ragwort plants. But the caterpillars we took to be those of the burnets weren't that at all. The black-and-yellow caterpillars belong to a completely different species, the cinnabar moth. We sometimes saw adult cinnabars flying, though rarely compared to the burnets. Cinnabar pupae are a dull red-brown. They're swathed in a silk cocoon that's placed just under the surface of the ground, or concealed amid leafy detritus. I don't think I've ever seen one. The hidden nature of cinnabar chrysalises, discreet—secretive—compared to the obvious pouches that the burnets leave open to view on scores of grass stems, combined with the fact that the burnet caterpillars are hard to spot (they feed on low-growing bird's-foot trefoil and are well camouflaged), perhaps excuses the muddle. It was years before I realized our mistake in pairing as two stages of one species the raucously striped cinnabar caterpillars shouting their existence from tall ragwort plants and the similarly loudly painted burnet moths. We simply failed to notice the utterly nongarish burnet caterpillars feeding unobtrusively at our feet, or the hidden chrysalises that cinnabars pupate into.

Thinking about the vanished Picts, I wonder if, in a similar manner, I've linked the staring-me-in-the-face evidence of their absence and annihilation to obvious verdicts about human finitude, while missing subtler seams of evidence that might be suggestive of quite different meanings.

Picturing the Day

Every morning before breakfast I look at the picture that's given on my page-a-day art calendar. This means moving yesterday's picture to the back of the block of loose-leaf pages that are held in a plastic display stand, so that the picture behind it is revealed. After six months, the whole block of pages is lifted out and turned round. The obverse side provides the images for the second half of the year.

Usually, the day's picture is a painting, though sometimes it's an object or a photograph. Often, what's been chosen is by a famous artist, but not infrequently there are works by people I've never heard of. The images can be ancient or modern, and although Western art predominates, there's material from other cultures too. One of my daughters gave me my first page-a-day calendar as a Christmas present about half-a-dozen years ago. It had an immediate appeal that's never faded. I've bought one every year since then. It's become a small part of the way in which I start my day, something that's taken on sufficient importance that I miss it when I'm away. It's become so much a part of normal that its absence now feels strange.

The publisher's blurb on the cardboard sleeve the calendar comes packaged in contains more truth than is usual with advertising patter. "Turn your desktop into a museum of fine art." "This calendar is a gallery for your desk." Well, I keep it on a shelf in the kitchen, a room that I'm in no risk of mistaking for a museum or gallery. But for all the hyperbole, yes, I do find "beauty, inspiration and delight" in it, the three words used as a banner headline above the promotional spiel.

There's a narrow border across the top of every page. In this is printed the day's date and a caption for the picture. The caption gives the artist's name and dates of birth and death, the title of the work, when it was completed, the medium in which it's executed, and where it's held. This is usually one of the world's great galleries or museums, but sometimes ownership is attributed to some obscure provincial venue or a private collection. Often, only a detail of a painting is shown in the main picture, which takes up all the page below the caption. In that case, (*detail*) is printed beside the title and a thumbnail of the entire thing is given at the top right, beside the date. This is just large enough to see the nature of the excerpt. On the day that I'm writing this paragraph the calendar's caption says: "17 February. Wednesday. 2021. Paul Signac (1863–1935). *Notre Dame*, 1885. Watercolour on paper. Private collection."

* * *

It's the image for the day I look forward to seeing when I turn to a new page every morning. But the calendar also prompts an exercise in elementary mental arithmetic. Looking at the dates given in the caption, I always work out what age the artist was when they died, and how old they were when they made the piece in question.

These little sums are spurred by creative anxiety. I've reached an age where, as a writer, it's easy to harbor the worry that my best work may be behind me. I'm susceptible to a view I do not wish to hold, namely, that artistic endeavor—whether it's the composition of an essay or the painting of a picture—is something that's done best in one's prime. I know it isn't true that youth has an advantage (let alone a monopoly) when it comes to creativity; I know age doesn't necessarily entail any dulling down. But at some visceral level that's immune to reason, I fear as I grow older that I'll be deserted by the muse that, up till now, I've always been able to rely on. It's annoyingly easy to suppose that artistic ability falters with advancing years, that our creative potential at best hits a plateau, at worst enters a downward spiral of steady diminution as we age.

Given this insecurity, I draw succor from the calendar on those days when I discover something impressive painted by someone in their sixties, seventies, or even eighties. Josephine Turner's *Poppies, Nill Farm* or *Braid Hills*, both painted when she was sixty-two; Pissaro's *The Washerwomen*, done when he was sixty-five; seventy-five-year-old Lucian Freud's *Benefits Supervisor Sleeping*; eighty-year-old Sir John Lavery's *Girl in a Red Dress, Seated*; Louise Bourgeois's amazing *Maman* sculpture, created in her eighties. There are numerous heartening instances, but the Japanese artist

Hokusai (1760–1849) is my favorite. He provides a pinup example of creativity not slipping into age-related decline. In fact, with Hokusai it looks as if the usual gradient of assumption is reversed and he gets incrementally better as he reaches life's final years.

Hokusai was astonishingly prolific, with some thirty thousand designs to his name. But his most impressive output occurred in old age. His famous series *Thirty-six Views of Mount Fuji* is generally considered his most outstanding work. Among many other brilliantly depicted scenes, it includes that icon of Japanese art par excellence, *The Great Wave off Kanagawa*. The *Thirty-six Views* series was done when Hokusai was in his seventies. Toward the end of his life, he said:

> None of my work done before my seventieth year is really worth counting. At the age of seventy-three I have come to understand the true form of animals, insects and fish, and the nature of plants and trees. By the age of eighty-six I will have made more and more progress, and at ninety I will have got closer to the essence of art. At the age of one hundred I will have reached a magnificent level, and at a hundred and ten each dot and line will be alive.

However extreme and unrealizable, Hokusai's artistic credo identifies the kind of trajectory I'd like my work to follow. Far from old age entailing any dismal tailing off, rather than allowing a drift into the merely mediocre—just going through the motions and coasting down the final slopes—there would instead be a pattern of continuing development. Though I know it's not realistic, I'd like to pledge allegiance to Hokusai's steely determination to keep improving. It takes admirable chutzpah to dismiss whole swathes of your own output as wanting, and to anticipate better work ahead. But doing so, dismissing anything that doesn't reach that elusive goal of pulsing with a sense of life—each dot and line of it alive—seems like a good way of ensuring that you don't rest on whatever laurels you may have laid down in your youth.

* * *

The page-a-day art calendar is a treasure trove of paintings and other artwork. It may not transform my kitchen into a gallery or museum, but it very definitely provides regular aesthetic enrichment. I feel better for seeing it. In these Covid days of gallery closure and individual seclusion, it's become a particularly welcome resource. It offers a sense of communion with other people's creativity, giving easy access to a wealth of striking work. To start the day looking at a work by Brueghel, Rembrandt, Cezanne, or Picasso, or to find on the page an exquisitely crafted Japanese kimono, or, in a very different style, a robe from Uzbekistan, or to see looking back at me an elegant Thai sculpture of the walking Buddha, or a carving of one of the ancient Egyptian deities—the examples are legion—is to start the day inspired. The great artworks illustrated in the calendar provide a pleasing counterweight to the often-grim news headlines. Not that the pictures are always cheerful. A Hieronymus Bosch canvas or a depiction of the crucifixion of Jesus contains stark notes of torment. But no matter how dark some of the themes addressed may be, I find my daily dose of art administered by the calendar to be an essentially uplifting thing.

The calendar is filled with glimpses of other times, other cultures, other outlooks. It provides a range of keyholes, cut into different shapes by a range of artistic sensibilities. These give access to a cornucopia of perspectives on the world. I like the fact that the introduction to the 2020 calendar began with a quote from Edgar Degas: "Art is not what you see, but what you make others see." It's fascinating to be taken on a daily tour through so many different ways of seeing, looking at life through the eyes of a diversity of artists. Though I know it may sound like something trivial, this little ritual of looking at the calendar before breakfast has become a surprisingly important part of how I start my day. It constitutes an affirmation/celebration of creativity that helps to light my way.

Having looked at the picture, worked out how old the artist was when they painted (or sculpted, photographed, or crafted) it, and their age at death, I often find my thoughts returning to the image at different points throughout my day. I don't just think of the finished thing. Often, I imagine possible scenarios of the artist working on the piece, and sometimes (a somber fast-forward) I picture them in their last moments on Earth, looking back on—reconsidering—whatever artistic oeuvre they've left. I like the fact that in some nook of consciousness I carry through my day someone else's depiction of a subject, a moment that struck them forcefully enough to want to craft a likeness of it.

Sometimes the calendar's picture fits the season: a wintry scene for a snowy day in January, a landscape of springtime green for one in April. But for the most part there's no obvious link between the date and the picture. Thankfully, the compilers have mostly resisted the impulse to try to be topical in their choices. Apart from some lapses at Halloween, St Valentine's Day, and Christmas, the pictures are simply a sampling of great art spaced out to give an image for each day. The calendar has brokered some wonderful discoveries, alerting me to artists whose work I've never seen before and introducing me to lesser-known work by great artists whose signature pieces have such a prominent place in public consciousness that they can overshadow, even eclipse, other things they did. But most of all, I'm pleased when I discover fine work done by those who are my age or older.

* * *

Curing my creative anxiety is only one upshot of the mental arithmetic I do each morning. Yes, looking at when the artist completed whatever artwork chosen for the day provides encouragement through finding a wealth of counterexamples to the default position I'm prone to sliding into—that is, the view that sees old age as incompatible with artistry. My calculations mean there's no denying the truth that there are plenty of instances of creativity flourishing in people who are significantly older than I am. Titian, Monet, Matisse, Picasso, O'Keefe: they and many others were still artistically active when they were ten or twenty years older than I am now. If artists can continue into their sixties, seventies, eighties, and beyond, then surely writers can too.

But my morning sums have another more somber outcome. They underscore that simplest, most immovable of facts—yet one we tend to shy away from—namely, that life doesn't last forever. Just as for all the artists in the calendar, their birthdate is followed by a death date, so each one of us, without exception, lives between two fixed points in time. Our momentary phase of being is dwarfed to near nothingness by the swathes of time that come before and will come after, neither holding any trace of us whatever. The calendar offers aesthetic pleasure aplenty, and role models from my seniors to spur my writing. But it's also a memento mori, an aide memoire for the inevitable but unpalatable approach of my own extinction.

My calendar devotions—calculations—often bring two death-related poems back to mind. John Keats's "When I have fears that I may cease to be" and Philip Larkin's "Aubade." Keats's fear was that he would die before his pen had "gleaned my teeming brain." Dead of consumption at twenty-six, those fears were well-founded. But though there were fewer "high piléd books" holding in their "rich garners" the "full ripened grain" than there might have been had he lived longer, Keats left behind an oeuvre that any writer would be proud of. This notwithstanding, his fear of not living long enough to express the creativity that burgeoned within him is surely one shared by artists in any medium. Will there be time to forge into paintings, or sculptures, or poems, or films, or novels the things that stir us? Or will we be cut off midsentence, with a book unwritten, a canvas unpainted, a film only started?

Working out the artists' lifespans every morning makes me wonder how these individuals handled the routine mortal terror depicted in "Aubade" with such austere poetic precision. All of them—and each one of us—must face the truth that one day we will cease to be. Larkin brilliantly lays out the way our sure knowledge of extinction is at once recognized and denied. The fact of our finitude "stays just on the edge of vision, / A small unfocused blur, a standing chill." One response to this shadow-knowledge that haunts us is, I think, to want to leave behind an account, an image, a testimony to what the world laid upon us; to forge into the form of a painting, or into lines of prose or poetry, a remnant of ourselves that can speak our experience to others when we are no longer here, as Keats's and Larkin's poems do, as do the paintings of all the artists in the calendar, elemental as any outline of a hand drawn round with ochre on the wall of some anciently inhabited cave. Each one is saying, "This is what I noticed, this is what life was like for me, consider this piece of evidence."

I've lived for four decades longer than John Keats. I'm thankful that there has been time enough for my pen to glean at least some of what has clamored for expression in my teeming brain. My books are not exactly "high piléd," but there are a handful of them. I've reached a point where, though I could live for another twenty years or more, become as old as Hokusai, if I died tomorrow it wouldn't be a tragedy in the way it is when someone in their twenties dies.

In whatever time remains I'm keen to keep on writing. Where does the impetus behind this thirst for continued self-expression come from, the potent desire to leave on the page a record of the mind's impressions? Perhaps it's rooted in the simple wish to share experience, the same imperative we've felt since we first clustered together around our campfires. There's always been a strong human drive to say, "I found things thus," and listen to what echoes back from others as they listen—look at—our perspectives and in turn put into communicable form the way the world has touched them. We seem to be possessed of a primal need to share our stories, to explain how life has fallen on the nets of our individual sentience, to hear how others have felt when faced with the same things that we have faced, to compare experiences. Is it just a sense of companionship we seek, looking for the reassurance of the herd, to know we're not alone in what terrifies us, what delights us, what mystifies us? No doubt there's an element of that. But I think there's also something independent of any audience. In putting words on a page, in crafting my sentences together, I'm hoping to better understand—to mark and celebrate, commemorate—whatever aspects of my time here happen to catch my attention. To explain what, for me, it was like to be alive.

* * *

Sometimes I wonder which year's page-a-day calendar will hold the image for the day on which I die—this year's, next year's, the calendar for 2025 or 2030? And what will the picture selected for that date be? Though the chances are I'll be past caring by then, looking ahead now, if I could choose, I'd opt for something by Hokusai. Though the *Thirty-six Views of Mount Fuji* is his most famous work, and I greatly admire it, I have a soft spot for an even later masterpiece, his *One Hundred Views of Mount Fuji.* This is less well-known because it appeared in book form rather than as separate prints, and because it was in black and white not color, but it's no less brilliant.

From this series I'd choose the twenty-fifth picture in the first volume. I like it, not because it shows Fuji in the background with the sun behind it, in such a manner that it's referred to as "Fuji as Mirror Stand"—the round disc of the sun seemingly held like a great circular mirror, resting on the mountain's summit. Rather, I like the human bustle of the foreground, its down-to-earth ordinariness. Two fishermen are maneuvering their boat under a low bridge, over which another fisherman is walking home, his dog following at his heels. He has an oar over his shoulder, from which is hung a bottle of sake. As Henry D. Smith puts it in his commentary, "The scene reeks of humanity." The picture is full of life and so brings Hokusai's artistic credo back to mind. That would seem a good note to go out on.

Thinking about which picture I'd select as the image for my death day reminds me of the way in which Larkin, in "Aubade," looks at how an awareness of our inevitably approaching end can make "all thought impossible but how / And where and when I shall myself die." He describes this as an "arid interrogation," but one we're repeatedly drawn to considering. Certainly my daily calendar ritual often makes me imagine various scenarios for my own demise. The suddenness of heart attack or aneurism or accident; the lingering of dementia; or stroke-inflicted paralysis. A hospi-

富士百撰

talized ending with drips and drugs preserving and clouding the mind, or a clear-headed exit in the midst of familiar surroundings. And I think of the great Montaigne, who died—probably from quinsy—in 1592 at the age of fifty-nine. He said, in his essay "That to philosophize is to learn to die":

> And I want death to find me planting my cabbages, but careless of death, and still more of my unfinished garden.

I warm to that image in the same way I warm to Hokusai's credo. At work in the garden, planting vegetables, thinking neither of death nor of the weeding and pruning and tending that's needed elsewhere, but simply concentrating on the task in hand. Perhaps by then my back or legs or hands or heart will have made gardening impossible. In that case (and perhaps in any case) for *planting* read *writing*, for *cabbages* read *essays*, for *garden* read *book*.

Learning to See Goldcrests

"The hardest thing of all to see is what is really there."
—J. A. BAKER, THE PEREGRINE

I'm nine years old and playing hide-and-seek with friends. Their house is just across the road from ours. I've decided that the best place to hide is in one of the fir trees that grow in a tightly packed line marking the boundary between their garden and the pavement. I choose a tree and, as I climb, look across the road and see glimpses of my own house and garden from a new perspective. Halfway up I pause to take in this unaccustomed view. What's so familiar appears strangely different from my elevated vantage point. Then I resume my climb. That's when I see it, just above me, an exquisite, mossy orb in greens and yellows, spangled with a dusting of white and silver. It's about the size of an orange, pendulously graceful, slung from the end of a branch that's too thin to take my weight.

My first thought is that the tree has sprouted a secret fruit, enticingly within reach, plump with the promise of its ripeness. But I soon dismiss *fruit* as too ordinary a word to catch it. It seems more like some intimate arboreal essence budded into being, the spirit of the tree's sap and heartwood given form. It feels as if I've stumbled on a fir-soul made manifest, hidden behind the shielding of the foliage. As I look, the fact that it's something crafted becomes apparent, though it's easy to see why I mistook it for an integral part of the tree. The perfection of the construction and the natural materials used give it the semblance of something living. The white-and-silver dusting is the gossamer of cobwebs, a network of binding filaments woven through the structure, holding its substance together and securing it to the branch from which it's hanging. Even at a glance, the softness of the gathered moss is evident. It's as if the eyes can feel the quality it would have if touched. The blended greens and yellows announce their tactile quality as surely as if it was another color. But there's an element of tensile strength as well. Examined closely, I can see wiry fragments of lichen embedded in the moss, like strands of chainmail.

The cupped shape, hidden from below, becomes more evident as I pull myself level with it. The fact dawns on me that this is a cushioned capsule designed to hold treasure, rather than being that treasure itself. If any doubt remained that I'd found a gem of a bird's nest, it's dispelled by the appearance of its builder. On a branch just above me, no more than an arm's length away, a tiny bird appears. It angrily scolds my intrusion into its domain. I recognize it immediately as a goldcrest. I've never been so close to one before. I can see its throat vibrating as the shrill notes sound, denting the green plumage in time to their insistent rhythm. Judging by the fiery orange center of the crest, this one is a male. Females' crests are pure yellow. I wonder if his mate is sitting out of sight, deep within the snugness of the mossy orb. Unlike many birds, the female goldcrest isn't easily frightened from the nest; she sits tight in the face of all but the most extreme disturbance.

I'm amazed at the bird's tininess, its perfection, and its fearless determination to object to the giant animal that has lumbered its way threateningly close to the sanctuary of the nest. I feel a keen sense of trespass. Savoring a last look at bird and nest, I descend as quickly and quietly as I can—and am promptly caught. My hide-and-seek playing companions laugh delightedly at my ineptitude. I mention the nest to no one and don't go back to it. But in the days that follow I keep watch on the tree from our side of the road. In due course I'm rewarded when I see a peppering of tiny birds darting in and out of the topmost branches like sprays of catapulted seeds.

* * *

The fact that I remember it so clearly is testimony to the power of this cameo scene from childhood. For all its mossy softness, the nest hit me like a meteorite and left my remembrance cratered with its impact. In the instant of the moment's unfolding I was struck by the beauty of bird and nest. But I had no idea then that it would leave such a lasting mark. Nor, as an entranced nine-year-old, did I realize how much I didn't see. Of course I knew what it was. I was able to name it. In those days children enjoyed a degree of freedom few are allowed today. My little band of friends and I routinely played in the fields and woods around where we lived, spending hours beyond the reach of adult supervision. Did we run wild? Perhaps. But we came to no harm, and through the slow osmosis of being there and noticing what was around us we learned to identify the flora and fauna that shared—constituted—our little territories. By the time I climbed to the goldcrest's nest I was well-versed in the basics of nature's local curriculum, simply through daily immersion in it. This meant that when I saw the goldcrest I knew what it was in a way I fear many kids today would not. It's sad that so many of them grow up in surroundings that have been despoiled, impoverished. As a result, the lessons nature holds are bleak. Increasingly, it's the curriculum of loss that dominates.

Being able to identify a bird is at one level laudable. Having the vocabulary to name things helps us to see what's there. But often the names we use have an air of dismissal as well as identification. You affix them like a label and that's that, the matter's closed and our attention moves on to something else. It has taken me longer than it should have to realize what it was my childhood self saw in our neighbor's tree. *Goldcrest* alone grasps only the smallest fraction of it. It's excusable at nine to mistake the fictions of conventional description for the way things really are. To a child, our ordinary diction seems unproblematic; it offers a way to parse and catalogue whatever falls upon the senses. But as we age we should become more wary about assuming the adequacy of language, learn to see behind the simplifications it purveys. Too often the world around us is obscured by how we talk about it. Nature is ill-served by the categories with which we dice and confine it; it's left depleted, cheapened by our words.

* * *

The goldcrest is Europe's smallest bird. To emphasize this, descriptions of it almost always include mention of its weight, together with a comparison to help us grasp how slight it is. Coins are often used for this. We're told the goldcrest's weight is equivalent to a five, ten, or twenty pence piece, depending on what point in their typical weight range—4.5 to 7 grams—is being selected. Though I guess our familiarity with coins makes them a reasonable enough thing to reach for, beyond the raw equivalence of weight I think they bring the wrong connotations into the comparison. A coin is hard, metallic, cold, and dense—none of which are goldcrest qualities. Nor does the clink of quotidian commerce sound any note that's attuned to them. Perhaps if a coin was made of gold it would be on the right wavelength, echoing the sunburst burnish of the bird's name-giving crest, and giving a sense of something small that has high value, buying into the jeweled perfection the bird possesses. Ordinary coinage, minted in base metal, simply seems mismatched.

When it comes to conveying the breathtaking littleness of a goldcrest's weight, beyond the hard-to-grasp abstract of a number, I like Brian Vesey-Fitzgerald's suggestion. This is made in a Ladybird nature book, part of a children's series that supplemented our in-the-field learning. He says that the goldcrest "weighs only the same as an envelope and half a sheet of notepaper." That comparison, first read years ago, helped to shape the way I pictured goldcrests. I suspect it still exerts an influence on how I see them now.

An envelope suggests that the form a bird presents to the eye is just a shell, an outer casing, something that contains a cargo, a receptacle for carrying whatever's sealed inside it. It made me wonder what was written on the flesh beneath the feathers, what blueprint was packed into blood and nerves and cells, what secrets might be found if this living reliquary could be opened, its contents carefully unwrapped.

I realize now how questionable it is to think of birds like this, as if they consist of an outer husk around some inner essence, that the body merely envelops and transports what matters rather than itself being part of the essential package. A goldcrest is an integral whole, a single thing. How could it be separated into carrier and what's transported? It bears the cargo of itself, part of the bloodline of the species.

However flawed this envelope-inspired way of thinking about goldcrests may be, it does have one thing to recommend it. It nudges attention away from the imperatives of sight to which, as strongly visual creatures, we're so succeptible. Usually, our understanding of things is dictated by the eyes. This privileges the present, makes us focus on what falls on our retinas in the immediacy of lived moments. I relished the visual delight of bird and nest, and it's a pleasure that still attends my sightings of goldcrests. But Vesey-Fitzgerald's envelope and half-sheet of notepaper have been helpful as a counterweight, a corrective that makes me think beyond appearances. I wonder about the letters of this species, where their tiny individual missives originated, where they're headed, what's imprinted on the manifests they constitute, what saga is being told by the totality of correspondence conducted by this little life-thread.

* * *

It's easy to let the tininess of a goldcrest lead to dismissive assumptions. Surely a life-form of so few grams is negligible, unworthy of attention. Granted, it's far removed from the scale of, say, an eagle, elephant, or tiger, but is that any reason to suppose it is of lesser interest or value? In our assessments of the creatures around us, is there a correlation between size and worth? Often it seems we must imagine so. What else explains our attitude of, as Joy Williams puts it, "Save the whales but screw the shrimp"? One of the reasons goldcrests appeal to me so much is that they reset my attention to a scale that makes me focus on what's often overlooked.

And before we succumb to the temptation of equating the goldcrest's slightness of physical form with fragility, we would do well to note that they can migrate over impressive distances. Every autumn, northern populations cross the North Sea, seeking warmer climes as winter approaches. As ringing records show, goldcrests have reached Britain from Norway, Sweden, Poland, Latvia, and Lithuania. I've crossed the North Sea from Bergen to Newcastle at this time of year. It's astonishing to think that these tiny feathered coracles can safely navigate their way across the same inhospitable route plied by ferries many thousand times their size. The wind and waves are often fearsome.

Before we were able to track their journeys, it was thought to be impossible that such small birds could make a North Sea crossing unaided. So began the belief that they hitched a ride on larger species that appear on our coasts at the same time of year. This is the reason that goldcrests used to be known as "woodcock pilots." People imagined that they boarded the larger bodies of woodcock and steered these weightier vessels across an expanse they could not by themselves traverse. The truth is more incredible than the folktale that arose to explain it. Light as an envelope holding half a sheet of notepaper, goldcrests are yet capable of this daunting sea crossing.

Sometimes on stormy autumn nights, when the noise of the wind wakens me, I lie in bed and think of goldcrests. Their migratory journeys are mostly made in the dark. One study from the Czech Republic, monitoring their autumn migration in the Krkonoše Mountains, reported that of a total of 20,647 birds recorded during the period of observation, 1,444 were seen during daytime, 19,203 at night. Similar figures have been found elsewhere. The goldcrest's favoring of nighttime migration is partly because there's less chance of attack. The sparrowhawk, their main predator, is a daylight hunter. Seagulls are likewise less of a threat at night. But the most important factor is meteorological. As Frank Gill points out, the more stable conditions after dark include "weaker horizontal winds and less turbulent vertical motion." Also, the cooler and more humid night air "favours heat loss and water retention." Migration happens at night because that's when weather conditions are likely to be optimal for long periods of flight. I imagine goldcrests above the trees, above the waves, above the fields, above thousands of sleeping, oblivious people, tiny feathered morsels of life forging their paths through the gigantic expanse of the dark. It is an extraordinary feat of endurance.

* * *

The goldcrest's robustness is also evidenced in its prolific breeding record. Every spring, they produce two clutches, the second often laid (in a second nest) before the first brood has flown. Each clutch contains seven to twelve eggs, tiny pale orbs flecked with a darker peppering of red-brown marks. A successful pair can produce twenty or more offspring in a season.

Though severe winters may cause fatalities, they are well insulated against the cold and, as temperatures fall, the birds will often roost communally. Two roosting side by side reduce heat loss by a quarter, three by a third. A huddle of several goldcrests makes for even greater insulation, clusters of bodies pressed close together to create little communes of shared, life-sustaining warmth.

It's estimated that the breeding population in Europe is somewhere in the region of twenty to thirty-seven million pairs. Worldwide, the species is thought to number between 98 and 165 million individuals. The spread of countries in which they flourish is further proof of their vigor. These are birds with an ability to survive across a wide range of territories. Beyond the British Isles, where the goldcrest is a well-established and widely distributed resident, they can be found in more than sixty countries, including

Afghanistan, China, the Faroe Islands, Japan, Lebanon, Nepal, Switzerland, and Tunisia. Even though the goldcrest's population trend now seems to be decreasing, the *IUCN Red List* categorizes them as a species of "least concern." That title may sound demeaning, but it's one I fervently hope they retain. Their spread and number should offer some protection against the new lethality of the Anthropocene, but it should not make us complacent. "Least concern" does not mean "no concern," as the just-published fifth report of the *Birds of Conservation Concern* series makes clear. It notes that we're witnessing "a continuing decline in the status of UK bird populations." The goldcrest may not be one of those immediately imperiled, but—like every species—it must contend with the environmental devastation we inflict.

* * *

If my nine-year-old self had ignored the goldcrest's scolding and intruded further, looked into, even reached into that exquisite nest, what would he have found? Would some or all of the eggs have been laid? Would the female have been sitting? Might there have been tiny hatchlings? I remember no sound except the male's insistent alarm. But I'm not sure if even a child's sharp hearing would catch the cheeping of goldcrest chicks: it might be set at a pitch beyond what we can register. Certainly the adult goldcrest's song, like the squeaking of a bat, is in that first sad tranche of audio loss that befalls us as we age. In any case, even if there had been calls coming from the nest, they would have been muted by its mossy insulation and whatever sounds provided the white noise on that day, surrounding my goldcrest encounter with their unnoticed background buzz: my breathing, loud with the exertion of tree climbing; the soft shushing of the breeze as it rippled through the branches; an occasional vehicle going past on the road; the voices of my friends; a dog barking in the distance.

Had I seen any eggs they'd no doubt have charmed me with their perfection. I fear I might have taken one. I'm reminded of the story the great French entomologist J. H. Fabre tells about removing a blue egg from a stonechat's nest when he was a boy, and the mingled sense of pleasure and guilt that it engendered. Later in life, this "inimitable observer," as Darwin called him, reflected that the bird's egg is "one of the simplest and loveliest forms of life," its appeal lying "in the beauty of the circle and the ellipse." More recently, Tim Birkhead has suggested that eggs draw us because their "wonderful curves" possess a sensual allure. Whether the appeal of eggs is geometric or erotic, I know I was susceptible to it. I'm glad that on this occasion my sense of trespass meant I retreated before the temptation of plundering the nest's precious cargo presented itself.

* * *

By nine I would have had a basic grasp of the rudiments of incubation. An aunt kept hens and we often helped her feed them and collect the eggs. That, plus what we absorbed form the natural curriculum, meant that I understood how crucial warmth was for hatching. But what I had no inkling of as I marveled at the goldcrest's nest, was how all the eggs in it are kept at an even temperature. Her size means that the incubating female (females are the sole incubators in this species) can only have two or three eggs in direct contact with her body's warmth at any one time. What of the remaining half-dozen or more? Nest design helps preserve warmth. In addition to the mossy exterior, the inside is lined with animal hairs and perhaps as many as two thousand downy feathers. A middle layer mirrors the exterior, made with moss and lichens (but no spiders' webs). Many nests are also fitted with what Svein Haftorn calls a "feather door." Instead of the open-topped cup design of most birds' nests, across the top of the goldcrest's, feathers are often affixed, their tips all pointing to the center. This helps to trap warm air in the nest's interior. But neither the triple layers nor the feather door would be enough to ensure that each egg is kept uniformly warmed.

Bear in mind that the female goldcrest is incubating an egg-mass that's greater than her body weight. It's clear from Haftorn's careful observations that the bird's sensitivity to changes in outside temperature, and her response in terms of length of sitting time, operate with great finesse. The correlation between behavior and weather conditions is perfectly aligned. This, plus the insulated nest, constitute essential factors in the temperature control that's needed to fire the eggs to life. But as impressively designed for the task as they are, these features still don't fully explain how the goldcrest manages to warm all the eggs to exactly the right degree for hatching, and to maintain the whole clutch at that temperature for the requisite period (sixteen to nineteen days).

* * *

The final piece in the puzzle of the bird's mastery of heat management was discovered by Ellen Thaler in her work with captive goldcrests. She noticed that the legs and feet of females leaving the nest to feed after a period of incubation were bright red rather than their usual brown. This inflamed color soon faded when the female was away from the nest, only to blaze back again after another bout of sitting on the eggs. This led to the discovery that female goldcrests increase blood flow to their legs and feet during incubation, using them like thermal rods plunged into the depth of eggs beneath them. Thaler measured a significant difference in leg temperature when the bird was incubating compared to when it was off the nest. Thaler also established—by eavesdropping via tiny microphones placed in the nest—that the bird shifts the egg load with the warming prongs of her feet and legs, paddling through them regularly to keep turning and shifting their positions so that all are able to bask equally in the warmth they need (a constant 39°C) in order to develop and hatch the embryos within them.

Think of what's beneath the female goldcrest as she sits incubating in the nest. Within each egg, an independent exterior womb, a life is fusing together as microscopic developmental processes lock into place in precise balletic sequence. Tidal changes are happening unseen as cells differentiate and grow, sculpting raw organic matter into goldcrest form. The biochemistry of maturation always makes me think of fireworks, controlled detonations cascading and sparkling within the crucible of each egg. Beneath the hard cuticle of the shell, the catalyst of the bird's body-heat fires the yolk into new individual being. The first cardiac contractions can be detected just thirty-five hours after incubation begins. In the period between the first heart-designated cells following their structural pathways, folding and torquing into the necessary chambered shape, to the strong pumping beats of a hatchling's heart, this vital organ will have increased its size by more than a thousand times. A controlled life-storm rages within the calm confinement of each egg; the clutch is like a nebula of birthing stars, part of the galaxy of goldcrest.

* * *

My nine-year-old tree-climbing self was delighted to find the goldcrest's nest and see an adult bird at such close quarters. It's an experience I've come to cherish, and the charge it carried was strong enough to burn a facsimile of the moment into the fabric of recall. But the more I've discovered about these birds, the more I realize how little I understood what I was seeing that day, or on the numerous occasions since then when goldcrests have crossed my path. It's only recently, as I've started to watch them more deliberately, think about them more seriously, and find out more about the detail of their lives, that I've begun to grasp something of what they really are.

Of the world's roughly ten thousand species of bird, more than half, including the goldcrest, belong to the order Passeriformes (a derivation from the Latin, meaning "sparrow-shaped"). Any bird belonging to this order is called a passerine. These are the so-called perching birds, distinguished by the arrangement of their toes—three pointing forward, one pointing back, ideal for closing around the twigs and branches on which they perch. The goldcrest that scolded me at its nest had its toes curled around a fir twig, gripping in the manner this ancient design allows.

The fossil record suggests that the first passerines appeared around sixty to fifty million years ago, though recent molecular studies would push such estimates back considerably further. Whenever their exact point of genesis occurred, it's clear the passerines were born from earlier avian forms that evolved from the therapod dinosaurs some 165–150 million years ago. These, in their turn, emerged from still earlier forms, the stepping stones of creatures in the great flow of nature, eventually tracing back more than three thousand million years to the moment of life's beginning.

Goldcrests separated from firecrests, their most closely allied species, around forty-eight million years ago. Since then, the emergence of various subspecies in Asia, the Canary Islands, and the Azores, over the last two to four million years or so, shows how divergence and geographical isolation continue to act on the bloodline, molding it into new shapes. These tiny birds contain so much more than a glimpse of one suggests. Every goldcrest I've ever seen represents the present manifestation of an ancient lineage. It points back not just to the dinosaurs—a favorite punctuation mark because they're easy to picture—but to whatever life preceded them. It's almost as if these birds are embers from a fire kindled eons ago. It still burns brightly in them, the flame of *Regulus regulus* passed life-to-life-to-life as if through a chain of little beacons.

* * *

The word *goldcrest* tends to bring to mind pictures showing male, female, and juvenile birds in the way they're typically presented in field guides: clearly delineated illustrations showing the slimmed-down wren shape, each one clad in its livery of greens, the adults marked with the telltale yellow slash of crest so bright it draws the eye. They're presented on the page in poses that flagrantly exhibit their visible characteristics. This is what we label *goldcrest* and what, in ordinary discourse, the name is taken to refer to. It might also suggest nest design and color of the eggs, and the characteristic quick movements, how the bird darts and flits and hovers. Essentially, though, *goldcrest* means what appears before the eye. But the more I've watched them, found out about them, thought about them, the more my imagination reads their name as something that can't easily be pictured.

If we're to grasp what a goldcrest is, we need to pack a great deal more into its name, ensure the range of connotation that it carries is extended so that it echoes with more than a few of the obvious visible features it possesses. Sometimes now I think of goldcrests not as anything that admits of straightforward description and portrayal in a drawing or a photograph of single birds. Instead, the name hints at something fluid, a glittering filament that spans a massive temporal distance, ancient yet still dynamic, a mercurial rivulet of life. Held in its waters are the repeating patterns of nest building, egg laying, incubation, embryo development, hatching, feeding, growing, migration, mating, dying. These iterations and their variations occur over eons, obedient to the nanoprocesses and structures that are laid down in the cells.

Part of what a goldcrest is, is of course the bird you see. But it's so much more than that. It's also the latency of liquid preexistence, what's held in egg and sperm, and the sculpting of their union via the delta of tissue pathways taken as the embryos develop. *Goldcrest* means the flesh and blood that form every chick there's ever been, the marshaled arrays of cells whose regiments arranged just so create feathers, color, bone, muscle, flight. *Goldcrest* is the intricate interlocking of history and histology, astrophysics and anatomy, the forces that have created the semaphore of crest and plumage. *Goldcrest* is each fresh-hatched chick within each nest, the successful first flights, the flights that end in sparrowhawk talons. *Goldcrest* is the adults on migration, flying in the dark, high above the waves, the scales on their tiny held-tight-to-body legs a signature of their reptilian heritage. *Goldcrest* should take in the eggs so skillfully warmed in nests built in ancient forests millennia before there were humans to fell them, and those warmed in unnoticed nests in today's neglected urban margins. *Goldcrest* should resonate with every bird frozen in a hard winter, the tiny bodies falling to the ground as gently as leaves—whether in the Stone Age or next year—scarcely denting the snow, their deaths making only an infinitesimal impression on the fabric of the moment. They seem at once forged of something durable as steel, yet with an evanescence and fragility that leave them vulnerable.

* * *

I sometimes wonder what befell the goldcrest that scolded me, and the brood of chicks that hatched from the nest in our neighbor's tree. Of course they're all long dead. Their life span is brief, only between eight and twenty-four months. But perhaps some of their direct-line descendants are flourishing somewhere in the world right now, their hearts beating out their rhythms at this exact moment. Think of that. As your eyes fall on this sentence, imagine goldcrest blood being pumped around the maze-ways of veins and arteries, flooding through the delicate small-bored tubing of the capillary networks that percolate every tiny nook and tuck of flesh, carrying life-sustaining tides in regular warm surges. Or maybe this particular line has been snuffed out. Hard winters, sparrowhawks, cats, magpies, human encroachment on habitat—there are perils aplenty for them to contend with.

Thinking about what happened to this small cluster of lives, the possible fates that they encountered, makes me picture generations of the birds coming and going, blinking into life and out of it again as the seasons turn, the years and centuries pass, each individual following whatever contours of happenstance are forged by circumstance—the whole slew of interior and exterior factors that determine their paths through time and space (their bodily form, the weather, the availability of food and nest sites, the incidence of parasites, disease, and predators). I find it terrible to realize that, as with countless other species, the greatest threat to them is us.

How many generations of goldcrests have there been since the tiny heartbeats of this species first sounded in the world, millions of years ago? How many more generations will unfold in the years ahead, until the last ever goldcrest breath is taken, the last ever heartbeat quivers in the breast? I imagine a network of golden filaments cast through time and threaded through an acreage that takes in many countries in the world, the veining of existence with the presence of this species. If we learned to see them as they really are, might that not engender a sense of wondering protectiveness?

If I had to give account of how my life's been spent, provide a tally of the time apportioned to all the things that have claimed it, my encounters with goldcrests would amount to precious little. But each occasion has left its mark, meant something special, possesses a value that's not reliant on frequency or duration. I feel fortunate that I've been touched by them, that I'm not one of the millions for whom, effectively, they don't exist. It's sad there are so many people who have never seen one, wouldn't care much if they did, and would have no idea what one was beyond some little bird they couldn't put a name to. Not to know they're there, living in the world alongside us, not to grasp something about these beautiful cotenants of our time and space, seems sad, a wasted opportunity to come face to face with treasure, a missing of something that can inform and delight, if only we would let it. They are something incredible that invites amazement. Like so much that we don't notice, this one small bird contains a staggering multiplicity of things within it.

* * *

I'm lucky to live somewhere goldcrests still thrive. There's a healthy resident population that's augmented every autumn by an influx of migrants. If, as I often do, I walk from my house to an area of woodland not far away and just attend closely for an hour or two to the currents of life that are always flowing there, the chances are I'll see one. It gladdens me when I do; I'm disappointed when I don't. It's hard to convey without sounding disproportionate how much of a difference to my day a sighting of this tiny bird can make.

But my best encounters have all been accidents. The nest found when I was nine. The goldcrest I watched on a bush in my garden two years ago, feeding intently on something so small I could only infer its presence from the bird's behavior. I was able to observe it for half an hour, at close quarters, as it feasted on this invisible bonanza. And once, walking to the bus stop on my morning commute, I saw one hovering at a coniferous hedge. It let me get near enough to hear the whir of its wings. Judging by the shreds of moss in its beak, it was gathering material for a nest and, I think, starting to lay down its foundations in the secluded innards of the hedge. I watched it for so long that I missed my bus, was late for work.

My most recent accidental encounter was so oddly serendipitous it felt almost that it must be meant. It was, of course, just chance. I heard a soft noise against the window. Investigating, I found that two goldcrests, both females, must have hit the glass. They'd come down, stunned, on the flat roof of an extension. One, I gave up for dead. It was lying prone, a wing stretched out. It seemed crumpled, broken, and its breathing had been knocked out of balance, leaving it panting through a half-open beak. The other, only inches from its stricken companion, was sitting still and seemed intact, though dazed. Looking down from the window to where they were, their gold crests were particularly striking set off against the dark asphalt of the roof. The fact that it was a dull October morning also made the yellow flashes on the top of each head seem brighter than they would have looked in sunshine.

My guess is that they were migrants. I don't live far from the Isle of May where, in October 1982, fifteen thousand goldcrests were recorded, as European birds made first landfall in Scotland. That figure gives some indication of the waves of birds that reach our shores every autumn, albeit not always in such concentrated profusion. As they move further inland, seeking the wooded habitats they favor, their route takes them past my house. The dazed bird stayed for maybe twenty minutes, motionless except for rapid head movements as it looked around. Then it flew into a nearby rowan tree. Several bullfinches, which happened to be feeding on the berries, looked gigantic by comparison. The goldcrest's flight from roof to tree was direct, unhesitant: it seemed to have regained complete air-worthiness.

To my surprise, the bird I'd given up on, thinking it was fatally injured, righted itself from its splayed-out position. It then sat quietly for a while, scarcely moving. Gradually, it grew more animated. Head turning became frequent, as if it were checking coordinates, orienting its sense of direction. Now and then the wings shivered with tremors of exploratory movement. Fifteen minutes after its companion had departed, it too flew off. I'd stayed close, partly to make the most of this opportunity to observe them, partly to stand guard in case a magpie or a seagull might have spotted them. But I had resisted the temptation of trying to give them food to revive them, reckoning that any such approach would have risked causing fresh trauma to birds already perilously shocked. In any case, feeding a goldcrest would be far from easy.

These two birds flew into my window as I was midway through writing this essay. What are the chances of that happening—and, happening, that I should hear the noise and notice them? Their appearance was a reminder of the threads of life that happen alongside ours, mostly unnoticed, part of the astonishing tapestry of nature that's daily woven around us.

* * *

It would be foolish to suppose that the sentences we write perfectly trace out the contours of what's there, match our subjects point for point. Language doesn't work that way, however much we wish it did. No matter how carefully we craft them, our words can only give simplified pictures. The descriptions they let us weave help us navigate a way through life, but they leave out so much it might be better to see them as attenuations rather than accurate accounts.

I've tried to convey a sense of what a goldcrest is, beyond the superficial label of its name. But the most I can give are glimpses of its nature. What it really is shrugs off words, dodges efforts to contain it. I hope the glimpses I've recorded here, partial though they are, will at least have some incendiary impact. Too much of our language acts as a kind of fire blanket, smothering the wonder of what blazes beneath it, blotting out nature's numen with our dull nomenclature. The more I think about it, the more I recognize how incredible a phenomenon a goldcrest is, and how impoverished are our usual ways of apprehending it. Compared to what it actually represents, what we say about it, our casual "There's a goldcrest" when we see one, does so little justice to it that it seems more travesty than truth.

I marvel at what each bird carries, what each one *is*. Specks of a bloodline distilled and molded over millions of years into this precise shape. Each one is saturated with invisible coding that bears the skill to gather moss and cobwebs, make a nest; each one is equipped with a sense of timing so that it knows when to mate, when to migrate, how to create the ideal microclimate for the eggs. Attuned to catch the minute creatures they harvest at exactly the right rate to fire the intricate processes of their metabolism, the isobars of a goldcrest's inner weather are exquisitely aligned with the niche they've colonized so successfully for so long. Their ancientness and tininess prompt me to think beyond them, to picture other life-forms following their own routes through time as goldcrests whir and flit unnoticed beside them. The minute perfection of their form, the miniaturized heart-brain-eyes-lungs-veins, summons more gigantic things: eagles and condors, blue whales and elephants, sequoias and redwoods, the varied expressions of life through its stupendous spectrum of shapes and sizes. Whenever I see a goldcrest now, I remember John Muir's comment: "When we try to pick out anything by itself, we find it hitched to everything else in the universe." For all their littleness, there's a weighty sense of embeddedness and interconnection about them. As they use cobwebs to hold and hang their nests, I wonder what the thread of goldcrest secures, wound around the world for so many millennia, and what we'd lose if it was cut or unraveled. Looking at them, looking at us, it's hard not to think of precious and precarious being far too close.

Details of their evolution, incubation, and migration provide texture for wonder to get a grip on, lay down a bedrock of fact to ensure its traction comes from the grit of what's there. Far from being built on hazy imaginings, my sense of amazement at these birds is firmly grounded on what they are. I'm left reeling by the fact of them, by the timeline of which each bird is an expression. Seeing one, it's hard to credit that you're encountering a spark of life whose incandescence has glowed across so many millions of years. The gold on their crests, the exquisite balance of the intricacies behind it, have been present in the world across expanses of time that make their North Sea crossings look negligible, and in whose light our tenancy of Earth seems tenuously brief and recent.

I still remember the fresh perspective I was given by my childhood climbing of our neighbor's fir tree. Looking across the road at my own house and garden from my elevated position meant that they appeared in a new light. Reseeing the world around us, recalibrating the value we give it, has become an urgent necessity. We can no longer afford to keep seeing in the same familiar—lazy—way. Is it possible to use language differently, to forge our descriptions according to new reference points, so that our words create perspectives that are as eye-opening as the view from the fir tree was for nine-year-old me? If we could make a modest beginning, start with the magnificent mite of life that is a goldcrest, learn on the manageable scale it offers how to see the nature of nature, perhaps we could then widen that vision, bring other creatures within its gaze. Wherever that might take us, it would surely be preferable to the brink of catastrophe, which is where the common way we see and talk about the natural world has left us.

Litmus Test

When I attended the University of Edinburgh, I lived for a while in an old tenement building just around the corner from Lothian Street, where Charles Darwin had lodged at number 11 when he was a medical student. There's a plaque on the wall there, commemorating the Scottish sojourn of the great biologist. Unlike Darwin, who was in digs run by a landlady (a Mrs. Mackay, whom he describes in a letter to his father as "a nice clean old body, and exceedingly civil and attentive"), I was subletting from a friend of a friend I'd never met. It was an informal, short-term arrangement that suited us both. She was traveling in Asia and wanted to keep her lease, store her things in a cupboard, and have somewhere to come back to. I had reasonably priced accommodation conveniently close to the libraries I needed as I put the finishing touches to a PhD thesis. I lived there from May until December, then packed up my things for the interlude of a family Christmas in Ireland, before starting a new job in Wales in the New Year.

I remember locking the door, posting the keys through the letterbox, shouldering my heavy rucksack, and going, without any feelings of regret. The flat wasn't somewhere I ever got attached to. Its location was excellent—a stone's throw from the National Library and the university campus—but the flat itself was small and dark and unremarkable. It was in a dingy, dead-end cobbled street. The towering buildings opposite cut off any view and gave a sense of being permanently overshadowed. The tenement building the flat was part of dated from the 1820s. Five stories high, it was constructed of the same smoke-darkened stone that's such a feature of Edinburgh's Old Town, the part of the city around the Royal Mile and within easy walking distance of the castle.

Medicine wasn't to Darwin's liking and he didn't finish his degree. He was in Edinburgh only from 1825 until 1827. At that point the tenements around Lothian Street would have been new, their sandstone not yet smoke-stained. I found it hard to imagine the blackened stone of the buildings cast in a lighter hue; it must have given the whole area a brighter feel than it had when I was living there.

* * *

The time I spent in that modest second-floor flat possessed no obvious traction for memory to get a grip on. The half-year I was there saw me focused on completing an obscure piece of research that was of little interest to anyone but me. I wasn't in the throes of any emotional turmoil, nor was it a time of much social interaction or travel to interesting places. My days followed a quiet, mostly solitary pattern that might have been dull but for the intellectual excitement my studies held for me. My living quarters had little claim to being remembered—except for one feature. This left a sufficiently deep impression that I've thought about it from time to time ever since; it's something that, unexpectedly, has stuck in my mind for years.

When I say what it is, I know it will sound strange. To have this degree of impact would surely necessitate something dramatic. But what's dramatic about a patch of yellow lichen growing on the stone of one of the outside window ledges? There's nothing obviously striking about it. Yet in every effort to trawl those distant waters of my past and retrieve from them some semblance of that time, the brightest and most certain thing is always this patch of yellow lichen.

In terms of temperature, humidity, and light, lichen can survive in such challenging conditions that it's often classed as an "extremophile," meaning that it can flourish in conditions few organisms could withstand. It has even survived exposure in outer space. Given the impact this patch of lichen had on me, I've come to think of this toughness extending to its grip on memory. Somehow it survived the fires of forgetting that cindered most other aspects of those days in their nullifying embers.

I think the main reason the lichen had the impact it did was because it carried senses of time and difference that made it stand apart from the ordinary run of things; it lodged firmly in my mind as a counterweight to mundane measures.

* * *

Anchored to the stone, its slow, tenacious dynamic spoke of a tenancy that dwarfs our brief sojourns in the world. It was paced to a duration that emphasizes human transience. Lichens are among the slowest-growing and longest-lived organisms on the planet. One specimen in Swedish Lapland is thought to be more than nine thousand years old. Their rate of growth is minutely incremental—in some species as little as 0.1 mm per year. Their growth happens at such an infinitesimal pace that lichen can seem like something frozen; it would be easy to mistake them for natural markings that are no more alive than the rocks they decorate.

I knew that the windowsill lichen's beacon of yellow must have brightened that dark stone through years of Edinburgh weather. It would have been there long before the day I was born. It's likely to remain, much as it is, long after I've perished. The lichen struck me as a kind of pacemaker, a metronome sounding a very different tempo to my own. For all its miniature appearance, it carried an oceanic sense of time's gigantic tidal presence.

Traditionally in Scotland, lichen was used as a dye. The small black cast iron cauldrons that sit on three squat legs and have such a quality of Halloween-like witchery about them were the traditional means of boiling lichen over a fire. They were once a standard piece of household equipment in parts of the Highlands. Now they turn up in antique shops or are used as flowerpots in cottage gardens. I like the resonance that's associated with dye. It often feels as if the windowsill lichen has indelibly stained my memory of that time and place, shifting the chromatics of recall into a subtly different hue of recollection.

* * *

It's easy to assume, as I'd done for years, that lichen is a single thing, a one-species operation in the way of other life-forms. In fact, it is a cooperative amalgamation. As the British Lichen Society puts it: "A lichen is not a single organism; it is a stable symbiotic association between a fungus and alga and/or cyanobacteria." A fungus isn't able to photosynthesize. An alga (the same goes for bacteria) can't build a robust protective housing. Brought together, both problems can be solved. Lichens are a partnership where fungi and algae—or fungi and photosynthetic bacteria—merge and blend in a symbiotic cohabitation that benefits both. Merlin Sheldrake's description in *Entangled Life* (2020) helps to pinpoint the extraordinary nature of lichens. They are, he says:

> . . . cosmopolitan bodies, a place where lives meet. . . . Lichens are small biospheres that include both photosynthetic and non-photosynthetic organisms, thus combining the earth's main metabolic processes. Lichens are, in some sense, micro-planets—worlds writ small. . . . [They are] places where an organism unravels into an ecosystem and where an ecosystem congeals into an organism. . . . Lichens are stabilized networks of relationships; they never stop lichening; they are verbs as well as nouns.

I like the way the quiet, intrinsic collaboration that suffuses lichen sets up a different life model to the one we usually assume. Instead of singular organisms battling for individual survival, here is something that seems both two and one. Fungus and alga (and/or cyanobacterium) weave a fabric that neither of their single life-threads could spin alone. To the naked eye, lichen seems like just another unitary phenomenon. It's easy to suppose it's a single entity, in the same way that a rose is, or a dog, or a sparrow, or a whale. It's only under closer examination that its essential duality becomes evident, the fact that this is something spliced and bound together, a pooling of resources to the mutual benefit of all. The fungus gains essential sugars from its photosynthetic partner(s); the alga/bacterium gains structural robustness, plus access, through the action of chemicals secreted by the fungus, to nutrients leached from whatever anchoring surface it's growing on.

Here on the windowsill of this small, city-center flat, easily unnoticed, a close to perfect partnership had been flourishing for years—two dynamics beautifully paired, their voices so finely attuned it's easy to mistake their complementarity's flawlessly dovetailed duet for a solo.

* * *

One of the things I liked about living in Edinburgh was that the city hosts so many juxtapositions of past and present. This helped me to see beyond my immediate preoccupations. History was evident in many of the buildings I walked past every day. There were places close at hand that influential figures from other ages had frequented—John Knox, David Hume, Charles Darwin once walked the same streets that I did. The castle is a looming reminder of earlier centuries; the university is more than four hundred years old. But even these measures give little hint of the eons that lie behind them. For that, the patch of lichen on the windowsill—*Xanthoria parietina*, one of the commonest of Britain's 1,700-plus species of lichen—was a better pointer. According to the earliest fossilized lichens we have, this type of life has been evident on earth for more than four hundred million years. I was reminded of this ancientness whenever I saw the patch of yellow on the windowsill. Its slow-burning growth and persistent presence lit a kind of flare that illumined something of the reach of time beyond my routine human scale.

I know that lichenometry is used to date rock surfaces. This technique has become increasingly sophisticated since its use by early pioneers like Knut Faegri and Roland Beschel. The principles behind it are well summarized by Raymond Bradley in *Paleoclimatology* (2015):

> Once the growth curve for the species in question has been established, measurements of maximum lichen sizes on moraines and other geomorphological features can be used to estimate substrate age.

It seems fitting that lichen's slow pace of growth and longevity can be brought into play as a way of measuring time. But I'm less interested in lichenometry as a method of scientific dating as in the potential that lichen offers as a corrective to our self-centeredness.

It provides a model that suggests different ways of seeing, different ways of being, on a scale of duration that dwarfs our own.

Paralleling its use in measuring time, lichen is also employed to gauge another of the elemental features of existence. Litmus—turned red by acids, blue by alkalines—is obtained from lichen. Figuratively, a litmus test can refer to a whole range of things that are used as points of reference in making judgments. A litmus test provides the essential criterion for evaluation. Its outcome indicates an assessment of fundamental importance.

* * *

When I lived in the flat for that quiet half-year of intensive study, I sometimes wondered if the patch of lichen on the windowsill had been there when Charles Darwin had lived just around the corner. Given its size, and the slow rate of lichen growth, that seems highly likely. Why did Darwin not complete his medical training? Some of the lectures he found deadeningly dull. But witnessing operations was a particular disincentive to continuing in this profession. At the hospital in Infirmary Street, just a few minutes' walk from his lodgings with Mrs. Mackay, he witnessed what he later described in a letter to his sister Caroline as "two very bad operations," one of them on a child. He left before either was completed but—unsurprisingly, given that this was before the use of chloroform—he says that the experience "fairly haunted me for many a long year."

A much more palatable experience for Darwin during his time in Edinburgh was taking taxidermy lessons from John Edmonstone, who lived just a few doors down from him in Lothian Street at number 37. Edmonstone was a former slave. Born in what was then British Guyana on a plantation owned by Charles Edmonstone of Cardross, he was given the surname of his owner, as was the custom at that time. John was taught taxidermy by the naturalist-explorer Charles Waterton (1782–1865). According to Waterton, writing in his *Wanderings in South America* (1825), he taught "John, the black slave of my friend Mr Edmonstone, the proper way to do birds." John subsequently traveled to the Edmonstone family home at Cardross Park. On being freed, he left his master and took on employment as a taxidermist for museums in Glasgow and Edinburgh. He also engaged in private work. Darwin describes him as "a very pleasant and intelligent man" and says, "I used often to sit with him." He paid Edmonstone to teach him how to stuff birds. The lessons were for an hour every day for two months. Darwin became a competent taxidermist, something that stood him in good stead when it came to preserving specimens acquired during his voyage on the *Beagle*. Without Edmonstone's teaching, how would all those Galapagos finches, so crucial for Darwin's great theory, have been brought back home for careful study?

It pleases me to think of the patch of lichen following its own life patterns, slowly colonizing more territory on the windowsill, almost within earshot of Darwin and Edmonstone's conversations. Unnoticed, and if noticed easily dismissed, it was yet as exotic as any of the creatures Darwin encountered on his travels—a Galapagos-in-little sequestered on an Edinburgh tenement. When Edmonstone spoke about the jungle flora and fauna he knew so well, did it give Darwin a foretaste of what he'd find when he reached South America himself? As he listened, were the ideas that would eventually crystallize in *On the Origin of Species* (1859) already starting, lichen-like, to colonize his mind-sill, slowly gathering pace toward the theory that would rock the worldview of his time?

Waterton, Edmonstone's mentor in the art of stuffing birds, was responsible for bringing curare back to Europe. This paralyzing drug, used by the indigenous population on arrow points to aid their hunting, came to be used as an anesthetic, part of the move in surgery away from the brutal butchery the young Darwin found so distressing. If anesthesia had been available sooner, might Darwin have completed his medical training? If he'd never met John Edmonstone, would it have changed his outlook? What would Darwin have made of the fact that today, as Ed Yong put it in an article in *The Atlantic* in 2019, symbiosis is "considered the norm rather than the exception"? Yong continues: "Corals rely on the beneficial algae in their tissues. Humans are influenced by the trillions of microbes in our guts. Plants grow thanks to the fungi on their roots. We all live in symbiosis, but few organisms do so to the same extreme degree as lichens."

What happens depends on so many links in the web of interconnections on which we're held. Alter a meeting, bring forward an insight, change an itinerary, and a whole ream of outcomes may unfold quite differently. Might Simon Schwendener's 1867 announcement of lichen's twofold nature have been received more sympathetically if it hadn't happened so close to simplistically combative readings of the struggle for existence?

* * *

How do lichens reproduce? The fungal component produces spores, which are dispersed by the wind. However, as Oliver Gilbert notes in *Lichens: Naturally Scottish* (2004), "reproduction by spores is a risky business." This is because when the spores land and germinate, "they need to meet the right algal partner before they can form a new lichen." Given the uncertainty involved in this, many lichens, says Gilbert, "increase their chance of successful reproduction by producing special parts that become detached and grow into a new plant (propagules) containing both alga and fungus." The commonest of these special parts are powdery structures that release soredia—a combination of algal cells and fungal hyphae. But this mode of reproduction can also take place through isidia, "fragile peg-like outgrowths on the upper surface which contain both partners." Gilbert records that in a rooftop location in Edinburgh used for pollen sampling—to assess levels for hay fever sufferers—"numerous lichen isidia and soredia" can be detected following strong winds. Perhaps isidia and soredia from "my" patch of windowsill lichen were present in the air that Darwin and Edmonstone breathed as they walked to and from their residences on Lothian Street. Who knows—maybe their exhalations carried strands of lichen to new anchorages in the stony canyons formed by the tenements.

* * *

I remember the Christmas I spent in Ireland between finishing my PhD and starting my new job in Wales as a welcome interlude.

I traveled from Edinburgh to my hometown of Lisburn, where I enjoyed a few weeks of catching up with friends and family. Years later, when I came to write this essay, Lisburn happened to be in the news. Sectional maneuverings in the Democratic Unionist Party had forced Arlene Foster, at that point Northern Ireland's First Minister, to resign. Two figures who came briefly to prominence in the political debacle that followed were born in Lisburn. Both were supporters of teaching creationism in schools. In their view, the world is six thousand years old. It struck me that these politicians would benefit from exposure to the litmus tests that lichen offers. Its age might help expand their ludicrously condensed sense of time; its mode of life might provide a hint about what Northern Ireland's antagonistic communities need to do if they are ever to live amicably together. I know lichen is an unlikely political symbol, but there are worse models for a way forward than the symbiosis, toughness, and duration it embodies.

Remembering Stranathan's

"Memories are all we get to keep from our experience of living, and the only perspective that we can adopt as we think about our lives is therefore that of the remembering self."
—DANIEL KAHNEMAN, *THINKING, FAST AND SLOW*

It's May 2020 in St Andrews, Scotland. I'm sitting in my kitchen on a sunny morning in the middle of the Covid-19 lockdown. My wife is cutting my hair, grown longer than accustomed (or wanted) over these weeks of seclusion and social distancing. Her barbering prompts a memory I wasn't expecting. Instead of making me remember how she used to cut my hair when we were students, or think of the plight of my usual hairdresser—business closed and undertaking strict shielding measures because of an elderly parent's vulnerability to the virus—the rhythmic clipping of the scissors summons something far more distant. I picture Stranathan's, the barber's shop in Lisburn, the town in Northern Ireland where I grew up. My brother and I were regularly taken there throughout our childhood. The hair that fell around me then was dark, undusted by the gray that now runs through it. It's hard to believe how long ago it was that those two little boys used to delight in feeling the prickly stubble on the back of their heads as they emerged, newly shorn, from the shop.

I don't remember the name of the man who used to cut our hair; in fact, I'm not sure we ever knew it. He comes back to me in fragments. Much of him is missing. He's full-lipped, his most memorable feature, with black hair slicked back in a brilliantined wave. The breast pocket of the white coat he invariably wore is filled with razors, combs, and scissors. Once, when he stooped to pick up a bottle-top, they all fell with a clatter on the lino floor. He said nothing but simply knelt and picked them up one by one, carefully brushing and blowing the hairs off them, before replacing them in the same pocket. His complexion is sallow yet overlaid with the pallor of indoors. He wears more rings than most men did back then, and his shoes are sufficiently pointed and polished to qualify as *winklepickers*. His style suggests teddy boy, though he's in his early thirties and should therefore be, as my mother put it (disapproval clearly evident in her tone), "old enough to know better."

These remnant details only add up to a partial picture. If it was a portrait, most of the canvas would be blank. Such incompleteness is tantalizing—it offers a sense of this individual, but one that won't come into proper focus. Alongside this patchy recall of my boyhood barber, a much clearer image comes to mind that sums up the nature of the fragmented memories I have of him. I think of the candyfloss accumulations of spiders' webs that fur the windows of my garden shed. Their nets of dirty gossamer strands are like cotton wool thinned and soiled, flecked with an array of insect debris, a record of predation presented in a kind of dry pointillism worked in tiny body parts. What I can remember about my first barber is like these dried-up bits of insect—antennae, wings, mandibles—a peppering of particles caught on memory's web. There's not much left, yet the pieces still manage to conjure echoes of the living person, in the same way as the shards held in the woolly ossuary that crusts my shed's windows still summon whispers of the butterflies, moths, bees, and flies they came from.

Trying to reconstruct from these fragments a fuller picture of Stranathan's barber shop and the full-lipped, white-coated man who used to cut my hair, reminds me of a scene from Homer's *Odyssey*. Descending to the underworld, Ulysses meets the souls of the dead. Before they can regain their memory and recognize him, he needs to provide them with the blood of sacrificed animals. Only after drinking this life-imbued liquid can the dead be parleyed with. The blood restores a level of consciousness that allows them, albeit temporarily, to communicate again, recalling enough of life to connect with the concerns of those still living.

Given the mnemonic potency accorded to blood in the *Odyssey*, it's ironic that the memories awoken by my wife's lockdown cutting of my hair are focused on a barber's shop. Stranathan's had one of those red-and-white-striped poles outside the shop, the internationally recognized sign of a barber. Theirs was a modern version of this ancient symbol. It was fixed like a flagpole above the shop's front door. Encased in a kind of elongated bell jar of glass or plastic, the red-and-white spirals must have been electrically powered. Turning endlessly, even when the shop was closed, the moving helix drew the eye with the illusion of infinite repetition, the prospect of perpetual continuance, red and white appearing, disappearing, reappearing without end.

The reason for the red-and-white-striped spirals on a barber's pole is all to do with blood. The poles are often capped at the end with a kind of bowl-shaped cup—Stranathan's glass bell jar was topped with just such a device. It too is blood-related. Only a few centuries ago, barbers didn't just deal in coiffure. They offered surgery, bonesetting, and tooth pulling. Bleeding was relied on as a key therapeutic measure in the treatment of many aliments; barber-surgeons used to bleed their customers as routinely as they tended their hair and beards. The pole represents the stick customers gripped tightly as they underwent this procedure. The red in the spiral stands for blood, the white for bandages. The shape that tops the pole represents the bowl into which the blood was drained. Some poles have a second bowl shape at their base, representing the container in which medicinal leeches were kept.

Though bloodletting has long been abandoned by barbers, something curiously elemental still attended our visits to Stranathan's. Perhaps the skillful wielding of sharpened metal implements at close quarters suggested something less quotidian than cutting hair. Or perhaps the strange mix of intimacy and distance conferred a special quality, the way the hands of someone scarcely known touched our heads, those warm receptacles of what we thought and felt. I find an almost elegiac note accompanying the realization that the full-lipped barber used to touch the head that, all these years later, is writing about him and still holds fragments of him in the invisible embrace of memory. I can't help wondering how many other minds he's held in. If I could access the way in which all the little boys whose hair he cut stored him in the mazes of their minds, would that bring back a fuller picture, or just further fragments? And how did he see us? My brother and I were just two among droves of little boys brought in for haircuts. (Girls were taken to an upstairs salon.) He may scarcely have distinguished one from another in this crowd of juvenile customers, or perhaps he remembered through a kind of phrenology, his memory holding a whole array of contour maps for the different shapes of head he felt beneath his fingers.

Is there any equivalent to Ulysses' sacrificial blood that I could offer to the fragmented shades from Stranathan's that roam the underworld of my remembrance, something that might make more whole the memories they represent? I don't think there's anything straightforwardly efficacious, no magic pill, no obvious medicine to take, though perhaps writing this kind of reflection is a type of self-bloodletting that makes an incision in the psyche's store of what has past and collects what flows in its bowl of words. I'm not sure how seriously to take that conjecture. But whatever's made of it, there are two more prosaic strategies that can help.

The first involves an almost meditative focusing and disciplining of the mind as I imagine myself returned to that point in childhood. I think through the years, reach back and back again, try to discount distraction, let the noise of the present fall away until I'm there again in spirit. I hope the spectral touch of this kind of concentrated attention can nudge some of the particles of remembrance into new alignment, send a pulse of voltage through them so that they can come together, cohere into more viable patterns, even jerk back into momentary life.

The second strategy is more straightforward. It simply involves asking my older brother what he remembers. We were always taken to Stranathan's together, which means I can tap into a second perspective, access another set of memories to lay beside my own, and see what tallies. Using the whetstone of his independent recollection offers a way of sharpening my version of the past, giving it a keener, truer edge so that it can cut through the years more cleanly and see those vanished days again, cleared of the overlay of time that's passed since they were present.

Putting these two strategies into play has helped me to imagine going through the door to Stranathan's again, passing under the endlessly turning barber's pole. My brother and I are ushered in by a parent; we don't agree whether it was our mother or father who most often accompanied us. The three of us sit down side by side in the row of chairs arranged against the back wall, waiting for our turn. There's a warm, sweet smell of perfumed oils and lotions. As for noises, the snip-snip of scissors, the buzz of electric clippers, and sporadic conversation don't quite blot out the sound of clumps of hair falling on the floor in featherlight swishes. If you listen closely you can hear this gentle punctuation every now and then, making a sound that's reminiscent of wire-brush drumsticks touched gently to a cymbal. The single window in this back room of the shop is always closed. Its lower half is net-curtained, its upper half is misted with the heat of the muggy salon atmosphere, blurring the view of nearby buildings. On the windowsill sits a large valve radio. Is it switched on? Is there music playing? My memory is of it being tuned to a sports channel, with commentary on horse racing. But my brother doesn't remember there being a radio at all, so perhaps my mind has conjured it from somewhere else, and those excited cadences of the commentator's voice as the horses near the finish line are not part of the aural background of Stranathan's at all but have strayed here from some other fragment caught on remembrance's candyfloss web of pieces.

We both agree that there were three red leather swivel chairs, with silver levers for adjusting their height and angle. Each chair is facing a large, rectangular mirror. The mirrors are fixed to the wall by screws at their corners. Each screw is covered by the small domed globe of a shiny, gold-plated head. I'm fascinated by the missing screw at the bottom left of the center mirror. It reveals a small dark hole that I imagine some secretive insect creeping out of once the shop is quiet. Perhaps there's a whole warren of tunnels hidden behind the mirror's surface. When customers sitting in the swivel chairs look at their reflections, they can also see the row of chairs behind them where my brother and I—and often one or two others—sit fidgeting, waiting for our turn. Under the line of mirrors there's a shelf that runs the full length of the room. It's littered with combs and brushes, scissors and clippers, shaving brushes, cutthroat razors and the leather strops used to sharpen them, bottles and tubes of hair oil and brilliantine, all the tools of the trade.

Of the three barbers who worked in Stranathan's, we remember the full-lipped teddy-boyish one so much more clearly than the others that it's almost as if he's in color while his two colleagues are in washed-out sepia or black-and-white. He always worked at the middle chair, between an older, balding man (possibly called Billy) whose station was the chair beside the window, and a younger man about whom all that we can summon now is the fact that he was younger and of slighter build than the other two. He was so quiet that the silence could be uncomfortable on those rare occasions when he cut our hair.

Is it possible to be sure what's accurately remembered and to distinguish it from what may have been invented? By *invented* I don't mean something deliberately fabricated in order to deceive, but rather something generated automatically by the mind in passing without thinking, as it strives to complete the patterns that are hinted at, finding the missing pieces in the jigsaw of recall. I've tried to reconstruct a picture of place and people from the traces of them that remain in memory. But for all my sense of being there again, there are many gaps in what comes back, and I know that it is exactly these kinds of spaces that the imagination is quick to fill and gloss over, supplying absent detail that may not match the way things actually were.

I wonder what befell my full-lipped barber. In one sense I already know the answer. Since he was in his thirties when he cut our hair, he'd be a very old man now or more likely dead. A common fate awaits us all. In that sense there's no mystery, no enigma. I can be quite certain about the outcome. What I wonder about is not so much the inevitable conclusion of his life as its unique texture. What twists and dips and camber marked the unfolding of his days? I'm interested in the specifics draped over the generalities we all encounter—desire, pleasure, pain, fear, regret, longing, satisfaction (our whole repertoire of feelings), the particular weave of one person's fabric of experience that results in the precise contours of the peaks and troughs that shape the map of who they are, the seismograph that marks the meanderings and undulations of the paths they followed. And this is precisely what's lost, or what in truth was never known. For even as we watched him in the mirror as he cut our hair, we knew little more about him than what's suggested by the fragments lodged in memory, fragments that seem so hollowed out and substanceless that they recall the husks of insects in a spider's web. Memory has preserved a sliver of what only ever was a sliver. The intimate texture of his life was invisible to us then and is now vanished beyond hope of any full-blooded retrieval.

How memory operates is something that has fascinated me for years. It's easy enough to see why some things are retained—they fall upon us with such force that we're permanently imprinted with their signature. But with others there's often no obvious reason why the mind has latched on to them and preserved them from forgetting. Clearly it would be impossible, and undesirable, to remember everything. We'd soon capsize under the weight of such a cargo. But it's often hard to fathom what criteria have been applied so that some things are salvaged and others cast aside. What algorithm was in play to result in the few details of my full-lipped barber being kept, while everything else about him was let go?

As I'm writing these reflections I remember the expression *harking back*. It means to turn back to an earlier topic or circumstance, to go back to something as origin or source. It stems from *hark*, an ancient word meaning to listen. Originally, it was a call used in hunting. The master of a hunt might shout, "Hark forward!" or "Hark back!" directing hounds and hunters to where it seemed the quarry's trail was strongest. The cries became set phrases. A hark back is a retracing of a route, a turning back along the course a hunt has followed to try to find the scent again. From its use in hunting, figurative meanings soon developed. I've directed the hounds of memory to hark back to Stranathan's. But the dogs are tired. Beside them run the unruly mongrels of the imagination. The scent has all but gone and I worry that I'll end up chasing something that was never there.

If I'm not to end up with a hybrid—a chimera—where garden shed cobwebs and the barber of my childhood merge into a single macabre figure, I need to keep apart the strands of memory from those woven by the imagination to create a metaphor that shows what this particular instance of remembering is like. The full-lipped, teddy-boyish barber is remembered. The open fibrous sarcophagus of the garden shed cobwebs is something pressed into service as an image that represents the nature of the remembering in which he's held. Or to use a different image, what's left of him is like shrapnel created by the detonation of moments exploded long ago as they came into what was then the full glare of my present experience. I'm not sure how feasible it is to reconstruct from these fragments an accurate sense of the force of the present as it lit my youthful consciousness back then. Can I regain anything of the luminescence of its immediacy, the bright light of its passing, as it struck me all those years ago? However much I reach back through the psyche's store of memories, however much I check the details against what my brother recalls, there's a sense of an elusive something that has slipped away, or that perhaps was never there in the way I now imagine it.

We know so little of each other. What did my full-lipped barber feel when he woke in the middle of the night and looked out at the stars? What did he most desire? What was his idea of a perfect day? What was he proud of? What made him ashamed? Who was the person he loved most in all the world? Was the gap between how he wanted his life to unfold and how it did unfold such as to allow contentment to warm his psyche, or did it breed the acid of resentment, regret, and disappointment? How far could he be trusted, relied upon? Had his heart ever held hatred in it? Was he loved? Had he ever written a poem? Listened to Beethoven? Read James Joyce? What favorite places soothed his spirit and made him feel at home? What was the last dream he ever dreamed, who was the last person he ever thought of?

Stranathan's has long closed. Its premises have seen various other businesses come and go. A gap of decades yawns between now and when the full-lipped barber cut the hair of the little boy I was. Thinking myself back and talking with my brother has led to a sense of the place flickering into the light of consciousness again. A great deal has of course been lost; there are many gaps in the picture I can summon, and I have no sacrificial blood to revive the shades that stir in memory's underworld. Yet despite this, I find to my surprise that underlying all the loss and absence and forgetting, all the uncertainty, I can still savor a feeling of being there. A sense of the place's atmosphere has been rekindled; I can feel its notes playing out excerpts of a signature tune I recognize, sounding in the same register I used to hear back then. In the end, the strongest image that remembering Stranathan's leaves in mind is of a barber's pole, turning and turning without end, bright with the possibility of retrieval and meaning.

Note

Red and white are the traditional colors for barbers' poles in Europe. The addition of blue in America is variously explained. Some suggest it stemmed from patriotic motives, introducing blue so that the pole echoes the colors of the U.S. flag. Others say it's an extension of the original symbolism with blue representing the color of veins opened during bloodletting.

Snowglobe Coordinates

When I visit somewhere new, I like to find one of those publicly displayed maps of the area that has "You Are Here" clearly marked on it. An arrow, cross, or dot—often in red—indicates the spot where you're standing, looking at what's shown and trying to get your bearings. Sometimes they're so faded it's hard to make out the detail. Sometimes the scrawls and gouges of graffiti render them useless. But despite their vulnerability to aging, vandalism, and weather, and although their fixed perspectives may seem primitive compared to the navigational capabilities of mobile phones, I still find such "You Are Here" maps appealing. I like them partly for their obvious utility—they offer a rapid means of gaining a sense of orientation. But their main appeal, for me, lies in another direction entirely: I enjoy the sense of existential absurdity they engender.

"You Are Here" maps offer a reassuringly straightforward understanding of your whereabouts. They plot your position according to a few readily recognized points of reference. Once you've scanned your surroundings, noted key features, matched landscape to map-scape, understood the scale and symbols being used, a sense of knowing where you are is fostered. This provides sufficient confidence to set off and get successfully from a to b to c. If these maps had a voice their tone would be like a newsreader's—calm, unhurried, authoritative. Their assertion of "You Are Here" invites neither doubt nor questioning. To ask "Where?" in puzzlement or outraged disbelief would simply result in patient reiteration. Look at the arrow, X marks the spot, that dot shows where you're standing. Whatever sign is being used, it lets you see exactly where you are in relation to your surroundings.

In one sense, such maps are unproblematic. They place us in a way we can readily relate to. But their plotting of our location doesn't bear much weight of scrutiny. Beyond a superficial sense of direction, the coordinates they give are little more than flimsy fabrications thrown over the chasm of a larger truth.

I don't just mean that "You Are Here" maps are simplifications. Like any map, they're not attempts to replicate the area they show. Rather, they select and represent. A great deal is, quite deliberately, left out. If everything was included, we would end up with an unwieldy facsimile, not a map. The surreal impossibilities of such a thing—a map that reproduced a territory with flawless faithfulness, a point-by-point echo with everything mirrored in 1:1 scale—is nicely shown in Jorge Luis Borges' story, "Of the Exactitude of Science" (included in his collection *A Universal History of Infamy*). Maps are not copies of the world but readings of it that excerpt and emphasize, they show enough of somewhere to facilitate our grasp of it, without bamboozling us by including too much. In calling "You Are Here" maps fabrications, it's not cartography's necessary simplification that I have in mind. I'm thinking, rather, of the absence of any indication that there's a great deal more to the story than the tiny part of it they tell.

It's easy to be taken in, to confer upon such maps a degree of certainty they really don't possess. We assume the little fictions that they offer are straightforward facts, slip too readily into thinking that their version of our whereabouts is accurate, that we can accept where they place us as truthful snapshots of where we actually are. Yes, of course, they do provide some passing sense of orientation; they help us find our way around whatever area they're concerned with. But the pinpointing they offer is fractional, provisional, temporary at best. It gives no sense of the fundamental nature of our surroundings, or their scale, or where we fit into the astonishing picture they are part of.

* * *

When I'm musing about the nature of "You Are Here" maps, I often think of snowglobes. A snowglobe is a small transparent sphere of glass or plastic. Within its dome, some miniaturized scene is depicted—a village or a farmyard, a city street, a little rural landscape with hills and trees. Usually a few figures are included, sometimes animals as well. Model vehicles are often placed in urban scenes.

Snowglobes are particularly popular at Christmas. Then, their cameos take on a seasonal theme—horse-drawn sledges, red-robed Santa Clauses, snowmen, reindeer, Christmas trees. The space enclosed within the snowglobe's dome is filled with clear liquid and scores of tiny white particles. When the globe is shaken, the particles are agitated and give the impression of a flurry of snowflakes. They make their slow descent through the watery atmosphere that holds them, briefly creating a miniature blizzard-effect. Soon they settle and the scene clears. It stays that way until the globe is shaken again.

Imagine a snowglobe where a fragment of a town has been modelled within the transparent enclosure—miniaturized streets and buildings, with a few vehicles and pedestrians appropriately positioned. There's a tiny figure standing in a carpark, looking at a "You Are Here" map that's displayed on a noticeboard. If you shake the globe the usual blizzard would momentarily appear. But instead of shaking, imagine this globe is a projectile that's been fired into the middle of the Atlantic Ocean. The little "You Are Here" map that's within shows the figure's location with a customary red arrow. It provides the necessary orientation to plot a route through the model town that's built inside the glassy encasement. The position of anything within this sphere is shown on the map relative to the other features that the globe contains. But there is no mention anywhere—still less any mapping—of the miles of sea in which this snowglobe is bobbing. The depths and distances of the environing Atlantic are ignored. No hint is given of its powerful waves and currents. The few millilitres of liquid within the globe define the boundaries of its cartography. Its "You Are Here" map gives no indication of the megatons of water separated from its world by only a thin, transparent membrane.

Just as the imaginary map within this castaway snowglobe ignores what's all around it, so the real "You Are Here" maps we consult are similarly blinkered. In fact the coordinates they give are even more curtailed than those within a snowglobe drifting in the ocean. At least the sea, even at its deepest, is something we can fathom; there is the certainty of seabed somewhere beneath us. And, however far from them we might be, there are vessels, islands, coastlines—all known phenomena—that offer the triangulation of familiarity. There are also fish and whales and seaweed we can name. But the snowglobe of our Earth is floating in an expanse that makes the Atlantic seem like a dewdrop, and within the enormous ambit of what surrounds our planet there is little we can confidently label.

* * *

The Solar System gives a kind of stay of execution against being overwhelmed by immensities we can't map, it preserves for a while longer the sense that "You Are Here" is an intelligible concept, that we can weave a comforting cocoon of coordinates around ourselves. Looking at the Solar System may pull the rug away from locally measured estimates of our whereabouts, but it still provides a sense of what we mean by "here." In pointing to the sun, "Solar" brings with it a sense of light and warmth, the familiar feel of summer days. "System" suggests something ordered and purposeful, a pace of proceeding we can reliably predict and chart. Our family of planets orbiting the sun moves in patterns we can grasp. We can take soundings of Earth's size and position relative to its nearest neighbours. We know we're on the third planet from the Sun, 93 million miles from the fiery star that sustains us. Our planet is the fifth largest in the System. As names we recognize, *Sun, Earth, Moon, Mercury, Venus, Mars, Jupiter, Saturn, Uranus,* and *Neptune* bestow a sense of being in familiar conceptual territory. Seeing them written on the page kindles a homely feeling of belonging and may even provide a bulwark against what lies beyond them. But such reassuring resonances soon fade when we consider the wider picture.

The Solar System is just one small group of planets located in a galaxy called the Milky Way, a disc-shaped assemblage of numerous stars. It would take some 120,000 years for light to travel across the expanse they cover. And the Milky Way is just one among a multitude of galaxies. One estimate suggests there are at least 200 billion of them. They range in size from dwarf galaxies, consisting of just (just!) a few hundred million stars, to giants that contain one hundred trillion. There are more stars than there are grains of sand on all Earth's beaches, more than every speck of dust we've ever seen.

Cosmologists organize galaxies into groups, clusters, and superclusters. Our Milky Way is part of a collection of galaxies in the so-called Local Group. One of these, the Andromeda Galaxy (2.5 million light years from us) is twice the size and four times the mass of the Milky Way. The Local Group in turn belongs to the Virgo cluster (65 million light years from us). Virgo contains at least a hundred galaxies. But this cluster, gigantic though it is, is dwarfed by the almost inconceivable immensity of a supercluster of galaxies that's aptly named Laniakea (Hawaiian for "immeasurable heavens"). Laniakea consists of more than 100,000 galaxies.

The size of the universe—home to this plethora of galaxies—is not known. The possibility that it is infinite cannot be ruled out. It has been expanding since it came into being and is expanding still, which means that though it would now take light 500 million years to cross the expanse of Laniakea, it will take even longer in the future (and would have taken less time in the past). The universe is not a static entity. The flux of expansion ripples through it. It is not thought to have a centre or an edge. If it was possible to go in any direction fast enough and for long enough, eventually you'd reach the edge of the observable universe. Beyond that lie unobservable realms. They are so far away that no light from them has reached Earth or any of its telescopes. Who knows what such realms may contain? And if you travelled for aeons, on a journey lasting so long it would witness the birth and death of all the stars, it may be—if the cosmologists are right—that you would return precisely to the point you set out from. I like the way that supposition sends a shiver of locational vertigo through our looking at any simple "You Are Here" map. It gives a very different sense of the possibilities implicit in our present position. "Here" becomes a kind of portal into the mystery of time and space.

It's hard to grasp these stupendous astral distances and dimensions in any kind of meaningful way. They slip through the fingers of what seems credible even though the evidence for them is incontrovertible. They're not easy to hold in mind as features of existence, characteristics of the reality in which our lives unfold from day to day. Despite the massiveness of galaxies, they seem strangely insubstantial, almost spectral, haunting the edges of belief rather than occupying its centre. Though they are there, now, defining this—as every—moment, these Laniakean vistas lack the impress of immediate sensation. They exist beyond any direct confirmation from sight, or sound, or touch, or taste, or smell. I take Laniakea on trust from those whose calculations and observations have revealed it. I know it's there; I know we're part of it. And yet . . .

* * *

In their six-volume *The History of Cartography* (1987), J.B. Harley and David Woodward define maps as:

> Graphic representations that facilitate a spatial understanding of things, concepts, conditions, processes, or events in the human world.

Some indication of the variety this definition can encompass is shown in Stephen Hall's "I, Mercator," a brilliant essay that first appeared in the Spring 1994 issue of *Orion* magazine. Hall writes:

> There are maps to anywhere: chromosomes, galaxies, the brain, the cell, the spaces between atoms, cracks in the double helix. The edge of time.

With each of these maps, it would be possible to introduce a "You Are Here" indicator. But the coordinates it gives take on a quality of mirage as soon as we glance at what they connect to and recognize where such connections lead us.

Master cartographer Tim Robinson's explorations provide a rare depth of topographical and cultural insight into the ground he studies. In *Stones of Aran: Pilgrimage* (1986)—in a passage that surely applies to any map—he talks about the way in which his careful walking and map-making bring him into contact not just with the obvious ground beneath his feet on Ireland's Aran Islands, but with nothing less than "the network of being." It is a network dense with multiple nodes of interconnection. Robinson suggests that it consists of "tangle within tangle within tangle, indefinitely." Faced with such an intricate series of interrelationships—every feature, place, time, event leading always to others—perhaps all we can do is "tease out a thread or two here and there," as Robinson does with such engaging elegance. The tapestry as a whole remains beyond our grasp. As Stephen Hall puts it:

> The most important thing a map shows, if we pause to look at it long enough, if we travel upon it widely enough, if we think about it hard enough, is all the things we still do not know.

The same sentiment surely lies behind the famous line in Herman Melville's *Moby Dick*, when Ishmael says of his friend Queequeg's island home, Kokovoko: "It is not down in any map; true places never are." The true place of where we really are, beyond the snowglobe coordinates of our quotidian cartographies, is similarly resistant to being pinpointed.

It's not just a case of disorientation being ignited as our scale of inclusion increases, with distances soon reaching stupendous expanses when we think of stars and galaxies in their scattered billions. Something similar happens if, instead of looking outwards (Earth, Solar System, Milky Way and beyond) we look inwards. Apply microscopes instead of telescopes and you'll soon discover there's uncharted space inside us. Think of our multi-millions of cells, think of the atoms that make them, the electrons orbiting the nuclei, the tiny planetary systems of atomic particles that arc their transits through these inner emptinesses. Sequestered within interiorities we rarely consider are nanospheres laden with the potential to corrode the coordinates we use to plot our everyday positions. These nanospheres are as caustic to the certainties of straightforward "You Are Here" maps as are the exteriorities of Laniakean perspectives.

* * *

My own snowglobe coordinates are easily enough laid out. Like everyone, I was born at a particular time in a particular place. In my case in Belfast on a cold February morning. There had been snow the night before. The roads were icy. The perils of driving to the hospital became an often-told family story. There was a skid when my father almost lost control. When we passed that spot in years to come, it was always pointed out. I've often wondered what different patterns my life might have taken if the car had left the road. For the time between then and now, I could sum up in a paragraph or two the main factors that have given me my underlying sense of "You Are Here," that foundation-feeling of present consciousness that pulses out its guiding beacon of identity and location throughout a life. I don't mean by this any self-conscious effort at map-making, but simply the soundings of people, places, times and seasons by reference to which the contour lines on our personal sense of whereabouts are drawn. Wherever we happen to be, and whoever happens to accompany us, provides a background continuum of reference, creates touchstones that offer a sense of everyday orientation. For me, a handful of people and places—my personal polestars—have been welcome constants.

What I find hard to bring into focus is the relationship between my straightforward sense of who and where I am and the wider picture that I know it's part of. How does the spot on that County Antrim road where, as we headed towards my birthing, my father almost skidded, relate to the enormousness of Laniakea? Can I bring into any meaningful alignment the baby born on that February morning in Belfast with a bloodline that reaches back, through innumerable forbears, not just to recognizable ancestors we can name but to the crucible of creatures that emerged when life's presence first sparked into existence on this third planet from the Sun? Can my present point in time-space, sitting at a computer in an attic room typing the words of this sentence, look anything other than ridiculous—minuscule, ephemeral, insignificant—when it's put beside the immensities of time that stretch out on either side of it?

In one sense, "You are Here" is a simple matter. It's determined by the immediate coordinates—geographical, social, psychological—that define our place and person at any given moment. But there is so much more looming beyond such simple pictures. Even the sketchiest knowledge of it creates such a magnification that ordinary coordinates risk being crushed in the massive atmospheres of cognitive pressure that result. Sometimes I picture myself standing in front of some straightforward "You Are Here" map in a town I'm visiting for the first time, but instead of it offering the ready reckoning I want, its snowglobe enclosure of manageable proximities cracks and I'm left floundering in Atlantic expanses.

* * *

In *You Are Here* (2004), her fascinating compilation of what she calls "personal geographies and other maps of the imagination," Katharine Harmon suggests that the urge to map, "like our opposable thumbs, is part of what makes us human." Not every outcome of this urge is expressed through drawing; there are thought-maps and word-maps. Our sense of where we are comes from a range of sources, not all of them obviously cartographical. But whatever form the maps that we rely on take, it's clear a need for orientation runs clamant in our veins. We are salted with a thirst to know where and who we are, where we've come from, where we're going between (beyond?) the obvious markers of or birth and death. I don't think that thirst can be more than momentarily slaked by the kind of straightforward coordinates "You Are Here" maps give.

Harmon's book presents a richly diverse collection. Not just maps of the world drawn according to expected conventions, but maps that make use of imagination, humour, fiction, that explore ideas, dreams, and emotions as well as landscapes, maps that offer pictures of our interior worlds as well as of the external landscape. Among the examples she includes are: a map that shows the incidence of Halloween lanterns in an American suburb; a map of air routes over Britain by day and by night; a map of Srinagar embroidered in fine wool on cloth; Edwin Morgan's visual poem "Chaffinch Map of Scotland"; Seymour Chwast's "A Map of Lovemaking," with the anatomy of a couple in coitus depicted as a contour map. There's a sixteenth century Tibetan map of the body's interconnecting blood vessels; prehistoric hunting maps incised on rock; maps of gene expression in the body of a fruit fly. Behind all of these maps is the urge to understand our surroundings. Driving all of them is the thirst for insight into the nature of the things around us, for soundings that will reveal, piece by piece, the coordinates of our whereabouts.

* * *

I like "You are Here" maps because they stimulate my sense of what I've called "existential absurdity." By contrasting their everyday positional parameters with measurements that utterly dwarf them, I can savour a rush of vertigo at the vast disparity in scale. Beside the distances I travel in an average day, the "immeasurable heavens" of Laniakea, seem somehow surreal. But there's another reason I like "You Are Here" maps. They appeal to me because they constitute such an obvious transition between reality and representation. The ones I like best include a representation of themselves—a little laminated noticeboard displaying the map is drawn on the map itself. This makes such maps feel like thresholds where you can almost witness the world metamorphosing into the symbols we use to try to catch and manipulate its elements. A "You Are Here" map pictured on a "You Are Here" map means that thing symbolized and symbol are for a moment co-existent, able to touch hands, exchange breaths, beckon us to walk between them as a kind of transubstantiation happens. Mapping, like writing, lets us translate the surge of sensation and information our existence brings, allows us to channel the raw impress of things upon us into tokens we can trade in the commerce of our cognitive transactions. This symbolic currency enables us to purchase some trace at least of sense—even if our little economies of scale are left bankrupt by amounts that overwhelm all the refinements and confinements of language.

Perhaps on some distant planet, in some distant time, there will be displayed a massive "You Are Here" map of such stupendous size and sophistication that everywhere can be marked, where the tokens of representation will somehow be underlain by a gold standard which means that they can be exchanged for the true coordinates of where whoever stands before them really is. It's hard to judge whether looking at such a map would do more to terrify or enlighten us.

* * *

I realize, naturally, that "You Are Here" maps are drawn for routine, limited purposes—to help us get from the carpark to the bank, or find the track that leads to a mountain viewpoint; they're not designed to plot our whereabouts beyond that. It would be unreasonable to expect them to show our position in the universe. They're not interested in galaxies or superclusters, but rather how we can best walk or drive between nearby locations. I don't doubt the usefulness of that. But, for me, such maps, as well as fulfilling their quotidian function, almost never fail to spark a sense of bizarre limitation in terms of where they say we are. Talk about not noticing the elephant in the room! You'd never guess from their little markers that in fact we're on the surface of a spinning planet, formed some 4,500 million years ago, that it's orbiting a giant burning star, part of a family of planets in a Solar System, located in a galaxy that's one of countless others threaded through the immensity of a 13.8-billion-year-old universe. No, you are here, in the carpark, 500 yards from the bank. It's maybe just a few minutes' walk in that direction to the leisure centre—but how long did it really take me to get to this spot? That question prompts the lineage of *Homo sapiens* into mind, the long bloodline of which we're a part. Behind any "You Are Here" lurks a journey that has extended over aeons.

I sometimes think of all the different "You Are Here" maps that must exist, how each person has a sense of where they are; our personal orientations of self and place. The maps we carry invisibly within us will be drawn according to the particular life-situations in which we find ourselves. There will, of course, be many similarities—because of the common ground of our essential biology—but considerable variation too. I sometimes think about my grandmother's sense of where she was, how she would have understood the "You Are Here" arrow that pointed at her life. I doubt if she thought much outside the territory of her strong sense of local and familial placement. Beyond the immediate coordinates that did so much to define her—living, widowed, with three daughters on a farm eight miles from Belfast—did she have much sense of her whereabouts? The unsophisticated theology that informed her faith might have given her a few Biblical pointers. But I think it's unlikely she thought of being on a planet spinning in space, one tiny particle in a universe of stupendous span and age. Even if she'd had time for star-gazing and daydreaming, astronomical knowledge at the time she lived was rudimentary compared to how it now is.

So long as we can get from one place to another in terms of navigating our everyday needs, does it matter what we think about where we are? How much, if at all, do our different senses of whereabouts influence the lives we lead? If you could lay them side by side, I suspect there would be significant differences between my grandmother's "You Are Here" map and mine. No doubt mine will seem as primitive to those a century hence as hers strikes me today. But is there any reason to believe that my coordinates serve me any better than hers served the life she led? I'm reminded of the passage in Sir Arthur Conan Doyle's *A Study in Scarlet* when Dr Watson discovers that Sherlock Holmes "Was ignorant of the Copernican Theory and of the composition of the Solar System." Challenged about his ignorance of what Watson sees as fundamental knowledge, the great detective's riposte is: "What the deuce is it to me? You say that we go round the sun. If we went round the moon it would not make a pennyworth of difference to me or to my work."

* * *

In *The Wild Places* (2007) Robert Macfarlane writes:

> Maps organize information about a landscape in a profoundly influential way. They carry out a triage of its aspects, selecting and ranking those aspects in an order of importance, and so they create forceful biases in the ways a landscape is perceived and treated.

I think Macfarlane is correct about maps creating "forceful biases" in terms of the ways we read the world. He warns that we have fallen under the spell of roadmaps. By ignoring many features of the natural world, they exert "distortive pressure" on the imagination. The land is seen "only as a context for motorized transport" —an outlook that promotes "the elimination of wonder."

Laniakean perspectives are a long way removed from any concern about our stewardship of the particular habitats we occupy on Planet Earth. They are seemingly remote from the many immediate threats that preoccupy environmentalists. But perhaps the usefulness of cultivating existential vertigo lies precisely in its boosting of wonder, in the way it can recalibrate a sense of just how wild the places are that we inhabit, however much we treat them as domesticated. Stand back from our routine "You Are Here" maps

—whether they're of a city-centre or a nature reserve—and think about where we really are beyond the snowglobe coordinates they give. Yes, that may cause feelings of angst and cosmic lostness, of complete individual insignificance, but it seems likely also to ignite a blazing sense of untamed wonderment.

Caging the Minute

We cannot cage the minute
Within its nets of gold
—LOUIS MACNEICE, "THE SUNLIGHT
ON THE GARDEN"

I've just got to the *t* in "McIntosh" when I hear the bus drive past. The sound travels clearly from the road to the attic, where I'm sitting at a desk, underneath a skylight window, writing a card to my friend Dorcas. The moment shimmers with a sense of its own presence and passing. It makes the mind's eye open wider and see a web of connections, its filaments glowing like tracer fire. This spangled incandescence could shoot its illuminated threads through any moment—every moment—it could be permanently there. But this is something I see only in glimpses, burning brightly for a few seconds before it fades again. No doubt this is one of the mind's self-protective devices. Being exposed for too long to the full glare of things might reduce (or elevate?) us to standing open-mouthed, stupefied with wonder. Custom, habit, routine—what we're used to—spreads a fire blanket of familiarity over things. The muting of the accustomed dims what dazzles; it stops from igniting into conflagration the combustible potential that every moment possesses, no matter how stolidly unfiery it appears.

Why should the sound of a bus driving past as I'm writing *McIntosh* stop me in my tracks and make the moment glow?

Who is McIntosh?

Why am I writing about him and the bus in my card to Dorcas?

* * *

The trouble with the rabbit I want to pull out of the hat of these sentences is that it isn't one. I'm not sure what sort of animal it is, or if it resembles any recognizable species. Perhaps it's more some kind of mutant, a mongrel mix of parts that don't gel properly together, resulting in some monstrous body lurching brokenly across the page. Whatever creature it is, I don't know if I'll be able to catch it, or if I do, whether it will stay in that form or morph into another shape before it makes its way to you.

I have the cage and table to hand—or will have soon. I'll make them from the paper of the page and the ink that's in my pen. What's less certain is whether I'll be able to lure what I want to examine into the confinement of the cage and put it on the little platform the table offers for display. To conjure such capture and presentation will require patience from us both, writer and reader. Making the magic work can't be done in a few short sentences. Hunting what I have the scent of requires a longer game.

A picture will help, and I'll use one soon. But it only tells part of the story. What I'm concerned with is in large measure nonpictorial, if not invisible. This is an elusive quarry. It needs to be stalked with words rather than an artist's brush and canvas. Although its footprints are everywhere, it can be remarkably hard to see, let alone catch hold of. The pursuit will require some stamina, together with the ability to weave words into nets, throw them with the necessary precision, and see what shapes are momentarily revealed under the draping imprisonment of their verbal mesh. We'll need to be quick. The nets will soon be shrugged off and what they held for just a heartbeat will run free again.

* * *

Have I lost you yet? That's not my intention. But I appreciate that starting with the *t* of *McIntosh* as I sat writing at my desk and heard a bus go past, then letting this morph into talk of cages, tables, hunting, and pulling rabbits (or more bizarre creatures) out of the hats of sentences doesn't exactly add up to the kind of beginning that's easy to follow. So, let's refocus before continuing.

* * *

In *On Writing: A Memoir of the Craft*, Stephen King's entertaining and instructive guide, there's a chapter titled "What Writing Is."

King gives his formula in three words: "Telepathy, of course." He continues: "All the arts depend upon telepathy to some degree, but I believe that writing offers the purest distillation." In other words, writing allows us to communicate mind to mind. It works over considerable spans of time and distance. What someone thought in the intimate privacy of their brain's intricately folded fastnesses, even though it occurred to them in Greece or India or China centuries ago, can be laid down in writing and brought to us today in London, New York, or Mumbai, as vibrant as the moment the thinker thought it.

King offers a nice example to illustrate the kind of telepathy that writing facilitates:

> Look—here's a table covered with a red cloth. On it is a cage the size of a small fish aquarium. In the cage is a white rabbit with a pink nose and pink-rimmed eyes. In its front paws is a carrot stub upon which it is contentedly munching. On its back, clearly marked in blue ink is the numeral 8.

Of course there will be variations in how King and his readers fill in the details of this cameo scene. We won't all see the red cloth covering the table in exactly the same hue. We may picture a cage made of different materials (wire, wood, plastic) and built according to different designs. The table won't be exactly the same size or shape for everyone—it could be oval, square, rectangular, or circular; it might be knee or waist high. The rabbit will vary in size, age, the expression on its face, the length of its ears, and the angle at which they're held. But for the most part, although we're not in the same place and not in the same time (*On Writing* was written in 1997), we all share a thought in common, which means "we're having a meeting of the minds." As King puts it:

> I sent you a table with a red cloth on it, a cage, a rabbit, and the number eight in blue ink. You got them all, especially the blue eight. We're engaged in an act of telepathy.

I like King's example. It's a vivid reminder of something easily forgotten: what an incredible thing writing is. With just a few marks on a page or screen one person can convey to others—across continents, over oceans, through centuries—what they think, feel, dream, imagine. We're so used to writing that it's mostly seen as something ordinary; it's so routine as to be scarcely noticed. But even in its most mundane manifestations what it accomplishes is extraordinary. Think of what the twenty-six letters of the alphabet let us do. With them we can mine our experience, arrange the ore of what we want to share in a way that makes it transportable to others. We can put a shopping list or utter anguish into words, use them to talk about love or how to install computer software. Through words we can express deep yearning, existential dread, describe a flower or the latest plot twist in a TV soap opera.

* * *

Conveying a simple scene, particularly one with deliberately memorable features, is relatively straightforward, as King's example deftly shows. But the intended subject of the telepathy I'm attempting here is no white rabbit. What I want to place in the cage on my red-clothed table, get from my mind into yours, is very different. It's that most real yet vague and intangible of things: a moment (which isn't really a thing at all).

As a unit of measurement, *moment* is elusively imprecise. How do we know when one begins, when it ends, where its midpoint is? And how do moments exist in relation to each other? Can they overlap, blend, merge, or must they always follow one after the other, "in sequent toil," as Shakespeare puts it, in a series of interdependent yet self-contained links all moving forward? How many moments fit into an hour, a day? Can we experience two or more simultaneously? Are there moments that come round again, so that they can be reexperienced, or is each one completely new and unrepeatable? How unique are they for each of us? Is it possible for me to share someone else's moments or vice versa?

Yet, for all their imprecision, moments are the medium in which, to use that old biblical saying, "we live and move and have our being." Whatever their exact dimensions and relationship to each other, they are the manageable units of time that let us bring the deluge of its passing into the scale of human focus; the temporal nests we briefly occupy are lined with their unfolding.

* * *

It's often obvious why a moment is striking: a first kiss; the birth of a child; hearing of a friend's unexpected death; witnessing a stunning full moon or sunrise. Such things possess an irresistible gravity that pulls our attention into close orbit around them. Our circling there acts to cut them off from what surrounds them, makes them seem like singular units, memorable in themselves, something we can focus on and mentally encompass.

But I'm particularly interested in moments that possess a quality that's somehow arresting although there's no obvious magnetism about them. They're not charged with beauty, or passion, or tragedy, or the electricity of any other easily recognized source of voltage, and yet they have the power to stop us in our tracks, make us take notice of them. These moments—and my hearing the bus go by as I was writing *McIntosh* is one of them—are imbued with something special. They seem to offer a view of the texture of things that's somehow more revealing than our ordinary outlook. Such moments feel closer to the heartbeat of time, fuller of the flavor of being. Listening to them gives a sense of savoring the pulse of existence as it reverberates through them, beating closer to the surface than it does elsewhere.

I realize such moments may be no more than the false summits of random selection, things accidentally caught on the flypaper of the mind's passing notice and possessed of no greater potential for insight than any other moment. But they *feel* different, as if they give access to a perspective that holds the prospect of seeing further, deeper, bringing into sharper focus our apprehension of the nature of being.

* * *

Like the eight marked in blue ink on the back of Stephen King's mind-rabbit, I would guess that *McIntosh* is what so far most strongly marks the moment I've been describing. *McIntosh* trips the reading eye with its oddness, acting like an unexpected dip or rise in the prose paving I've been laying. It's something that doesn't fit flush with other words as they take my meaning forward. Instead, it juts out with the questions that it prompts: who is McIntosh and why am I writing that name in the card I'm writing to my friend?

What I want to occupy the cage I'm making in this essay bears few similarities to King's white rabbit. It's real rather than imagined. It's also sprawling, ill-defined, and contains a mix of actors. In addition to the minimal list I've given so far—McIntosh, bus, attic, skylight window, card, my friend Dorcas—the dramatis personae also includes: a horse, several dogs, trees, two trains, a boat, people that I've never met, a view across an estuary that I can't see from where I'm sitting. And that's just the start. Things soon edge into vistas that dwarf all of these easily named components. Nonetheless, despite the lack of singular, rabbit-like simplicity, I hope at least a measure of telepathy can happen so that I can transport what's in my mind into yours.

* * *

Let me set up my cage and table again, provide more detail about what I want to magic across the time and space between us.

Every weekday morning at 0720 a bus drives past my house. It goes from St. Andrews, where I live, to Dundee, where I work, a distance of about twelve miles. Because I know the route so well, the sound of the bus sparks an immediate thread of recognition, a mix of memory and imagination. Hearing it go past creates an image of how the bus will trace out across the morning landscape the course of the road from here to there, following the precise kinks of contour, camber, and direction, each twist and turn, going past the usual trees and fields and houses, as it heads for the Tay Road Bridge and then Dundee city center.

I work part-time, so some mornings I only see or hear the bus go past; other mornings I'm on it. When things unfolded in my mind's eye as I was writing *McIntosh* and heard the familiar note of its engine, my thought-picture of the bus, the inner echo that holds an imprint of its journey, was a blend of exterior and interior perspectives. As well as the countryside it passed through, I imagined the bus driver and likely complement of passengers. This changes from one day to the next, but there are enough regularly seen faces to make it probable that the picture in my mind corresponded closely with the actuality that was playing out.

I'm not sure why, but hearing the familiar sound of the bus go past as I was writing *McIntosh* made me realize time's passing far more acutely than normal. The bus's noise underlined the moment, even as it helped to constitute it. The engine's note sparked a keener awareness of the nowness that it—and I—occupied. Its triggering of a mental image that held a distillation of route, direction, passengers acted to create an illuminated cameo, a kind of icon of transience.

A moment sounds like something fleeting, the briefest span

of time. If it was compared to liquid measurements, it would be a quarter-gill at best rather than a quart or gallon. And yet the invisible cargo a moment can carry belies such small scale. The mind requires little duration to formulate a wealth of ideas. They can crowd into a moment without filling it—there are cathedral-sized rooms waiting to receive them; time's interior architecture follows an aesthetic of space rather than enclosure.

* * *

McIntosh is James McIntosh Patrick (1907–1998), one of modern Scotland's most popular landscape painters and an artist closely associated with his native Dundee. A few months ago I sent a card featuring one of his *Four Seasons* paintings, titled *Autumn in Kinnordy*, to my friend Dorcas. Sitting at my desk under the attic skylight I'm writing another card to her. This one is of what is undoubtedly McIntosh Patrick's most famous painting, *The Tay Bridge from My Studio Window.* I've just looked at the card's reproduction of the painting for the umpteenth time and have resumed my writing, but the scene McIntosh Patrick depicted remains clearly held in mind. It's almost as if some niche in memory-imagination rearranged itself according to the contours of the painted details, creating a kind of invisible facsimile, an echo chamber where consciousness lingers, savoring the ghostly similitude of being in a place that I know well.

Writing in the card to Dorcas I'm saying that I thought she "might like to see another example of James McInt[osh Patrick's work]," when reaching that *t* in *McIntosh,* I hear the bus go past and the moment seems both frozen and on fire. I feel its presence and passing with an intensity I know will dim soon enough. Trying to catch it in words I picture it as a kind of firefly, bright with its own ephemeral luminescence. I follow with my nets of sentences, swiping at it clumsily, trying to do the impossible and pin it perfect and undamaged to the page.

This moment is nothing out of the ordinary. It offers no revolutionary cognitive breakthrough; it doesn't make public any shocking secret; it's neither a revelation nor a vision; it doesn't challenge some widely held orthodoxy. There's nothing stupendous about it—and yet its dimensions are astounding. In the few seconds of its duration it touches an array of markers that stake out a territory far more extensive, incomparably richer, than anything suggested by the bland circumstances of its occurrence. I may be sitting at a desk under the attic skylight in my house in St. Andrews, but the moment takes me miles and years away.

The Tay Bridge from My Studio Window was painted in 1948, but the scene is still readily recognizable today. You need to make a few adjustments to synch past depiction with present reality: the trains that cross the bridge are now all diesel locomotives, so there's no steam billowing from funnels; the small cargo ship that's just sailed under the bridge likewise has an old-fashioned air to it. Such tramp steamers have been replaced by sleek pleasure craft. It would no longer be usual to see a horse-drawn cart such as the one shown stopped in the road outside the artist's house; the pram pushed by one of the figures in the painting looks positively antique to twenty-first-century eyes. But Dundee's iconic rail bridge is still just the same, as are the waters of the Tay estuary it crosses.

The landmass of Fife on the opposite side has more buildings clustered on it than in 1948 but is essentially unchanged. The trees and grass on Magdalen Green match the contemporary outlook from the house. Dog walkers and cyclists are still a common sight. When I last walked past where McIntosh Patrick lived and had his studio, only a week or two before writing my card to Dorcas, I was powerfully struck by the similarities between what I saw around me and the painting that I know so well.

As Ron Thompson puts it in *Easel in the Field: The Life of McIntosh Patrick*, this painting "embraced more activity" than any other the artist did. I think it's because of this activity that *The Tay Bridge from My Studio Window* gives such a strong impression of capturing a moment. The trains crossing the bridge, the cargo ship steaming seawards, the cyclist, pedestrians, dogs, horse and cart, are all moving things. Though shown motionless, held captive in paint, as entombed as flies in amber, their stillness is replete with a sense of movement, it emphasizes the interruption of a flow. In the mute testimony of their unnatural stasis, these elements of the painting are eloquent witnesses to time's passing and the fact that it's been caught and suspended here. The artist has created the illusion of a fragment of time frozen, a moment perfectly embalmed, held in artful, artificial isolation. What was here for just a fleeting second as he looked out of his studio window has been preserved and presented in the semipermanence of paint.

* * *

How long does a moment last? Where do its edges lie? How do they fit together with what came before, with what comes next? Is there enough permeability between them to allow aspects of one moment to seep into another? Does it make sense to think of them separately, or are they part of a single continuous stream? Is our sense of them as small-scale, self-contained, multiple, simply an illusion wrought by our desire for meaning? Could all of history—time itself—be considered as a single moment, our experience no more than a handful of minuscule fragments taken from it?

The more I examine it, the more it feels that the moment marked by hearing the bus drive past as I was writing my *McIntosh* Patrick card to Dorcas was an entanglement of at least two moments—continuing (for the moment) with the useful fiction that moments are separable things. The view from the artist's studio window, painted seventy-five years ago, merged and melded with the present moment (as it was then) of sitting at my desk under the skylight window, pen crossing the *t* in the artist's name, his painting held clearly in my mind as the bus went past.

Thinking of two moments becoming entangled hints at what happened. But it creates too simple a picture. The clear-cut dividing lines it suggests would be hard to draw with any confidence or clarity. The ideas engendered by this collision and entanglement of moments spill into one another, draw the attention miles away, as connections spark and link with the speed of wildfire. Moments don't admit to easy circumscription or confinement. As they mix, the territories of now and then and next take on a sense of interdependence—interpenetration—that doesn't follow the contours of sequential commonsense.

The frozen scene depicted in *The Tay Bridge from My Studio*

Window didn't just transport me to that place via the artist's telepathy (for paintings conjure rabbits too), I also felt as if I'd fallen into a kind of time-shaft. Yes, part of my attention was focused on the surface present that McIntosh Patrick has depicted so engagingly: the late-afternoon sunlight on the garden, the way it shines through the trees, making delicate shadow patterns on the ground, the steam from the trains billowing into the sky. But the backstory and continuance of all the narrative threads that are shown stalled in his canvas shimmer through things and tug at the imagination. This bestows a mirage-like quality on the scene. It makes it alternate between what's shown, what would have met the artist's eye as he looked out the window, where the elements of it had been a few seconds—minutes, hours, years—earlier, and where they'd be as time continued after he put down his brush and turned away from his easel.

Where were the dog walkers heading? What stops had the trains made and what destinations were they bound for? What route had the boy cyclist followed to get to here and where was he going as his legs pushed down on the pedals? Where had the baby in the pram been conceived? What sort of person would he or she become as they grew into adulthood? As I heard the bus go by and my pen paused at the *t* of *McIntosh*, was there somewhere in the world the old man or woman that the baby became, nearing the end of a life that had been pictured in its infancy in the canvas?

But for some reason it was the horse that drew me most forcefully into the whirlpool of time that swirls and pulls just below the surface of what's shown. For it to be here, standing on the road outside the artist's house, harnessed to a fruit merchant's cart, think of the journey it had made. I don't mean just its plodding around the streets of Dundee, delivering a greengrocer's wares, not just its individual chronology from conception, birth, foalhood, to its workaday present and on to aging, death, and dissolution. That's an incredible enough itinerary, but it's nothing compared to the wider timeline it's part of. This reaches back, horse after horse, until it touches eohippus and, before that ancient form, the unnamed creatures that preceded it.

Horse, dogs, people—their presence at the moment in time that MacIntosh Patrick painted points back to distant beginnings, the dawn of life, the genesis of all our moments. The life-forms in the painting are like living clocks or hourglasses. They're shown halted, the hands on the clock face no longer moving, the sand grains paused in the steady trickle of their fall. But their stoppage, far from confining attention to a single moment frozen, made me imagine the hands spinning round, the sand grains not just dropping through the neck of an hourglass but falling through an immeasurable chasm, part of the flow of time before and time to come that surges unstoppably through any—every—moment.

When the 0720 bus went by as I was writing to Dorcas, yes, I was sitting at my desk underneath the skylight window, fixed to that point in space and time. But because of the meticulously painted moment in the cage of McIntosh Patrick's canvas, displayed on the table of the card I was writing, I was also in Dundee in 1948. That in itself would be remarkable, another illustration of the power of symbols, whether painted or written, a reminder of

Stephen King's point that "all the arts depend upon telepathy to some degree." But I was also far away from Dundee as it appeared in 1948. The time-shaft hidden in the depiction of the horse had pulled me into a bloodline that linked a moment that was only seventy-five years away to one that snaked back for millions of years. On the one hand, writing to a friend, looking at a card, hearing a bus go past are the simplest of things. On the other, they connect to wholly different perspectives.

* * *

Most of the figures McIntosh Patrick included in his painting aren't figments of his imagination. They're real not invented. The woman at the gate is his wife, Janet, with their dog, Lulu. His son Andrew is the boy on the bike. The man walking a pack of dogs is David McDonald, a Dundee stockbroker. The horse-drawn cart belongs to a Mr. Roy, a local greengrocer. They, the bridge, the trains, the boat are all rendered in realist style.

But I've often wondered how real the moment is. Was there an actual point in time when the artist looked out his window and saw everything situated in exactly this manner? Did he photograph it and work his painting from the view the camera captured? Or was it more a case of a moment based on (fabricated from) what he'd seen in multiple lookings from this window? To what extent is the painting a composition, obedient to the artist's sense of aesthetics, to what extent a verbatim rendering of what he saw? Is *The Tay Bridge from My Studio Window* a construction, albeit one built according to the lineaments of what's there, or a reflection of what actually met his glance on one particular afternoon when he gazed out the window?

* * *

I'm interested in the dynamics of what happens when a writer or an artist puts whatever rabbit they're concerned with into the cage on the red-topped table of their art. What do the choice of words or hue of paint, the width of brush or the sentences selected, the size of canvas or the length of the essay do to the thing they wish to convey? Whether it's something imagined or something real, it can't be the actual thing exactly as it is that's telepathized. It's not the cargo of the mind itself but a depiction of it in whatever medium's being used. I know that being caught in words does damage to a moment. It's not as if I can catch it perfect and complete and lay it down on the page exactly as I see it. Putting it into words is more like some clumsy boy catching an exquisitely beautiful butterfly in his cupped, sweaty hands. He passes it to your hands through his sentences. You may feel a flutter signaling its presence. But you know without looking that the wings will be smudged and crumpled. What will be left when you open your hands will be a bedraggled remnant of what drew the eye, an approximation of the original perfection.

The moment that struck me at the moment that it did, in the immediate vibrancy of its occurrence, the realization of its intricate, incandescent nowness, is different from the moment as I've depicted it here—struggling over days to put it into a form of words that works. My sentences may not catch it, but I hope they at least act as a pointing finger indicating something of its nature.

What I've been calling a *moment* is a thread of cognition-memory-imagination, a filament abstracted from the fabric of experience, part of my encounter with time-space, one outcome of my ongoing meeting with the world. It is the result of the catalyst of one personality reacting with the particularities of a specific point in time. But however closely I try to contour it in words, I know that what's traced out on the page will not be the thing itself. Magritte's *Ceci n'est pas une pipe* sounds a cautionary note that anyone engaged in art's telepathies ought always to remember, lest they delude themselves into believing that the world can become word or image without loss. That would be as absurd as thinking that a painted pipe could be smoked, or that the verbal description of a bridge would offer you a way to cross a river.

* * *

The day after the moment I've been writing about imprinted itself so strongly on me, I was on the 0720 bus again, going to Dundee. At the bus stop there's a postbox. As I put the card into it, heard it fall inside, it seemed like another grain in the hourglass, one that would fall for several hundred miles as it traveled the length of the country to reach Dorcas's address. I pictured her opening it, looking at *The Tay Bridge from My Studio Window* with her artist's expert eye and reading the few lines I'd written. I wondered how her looking would compare to mine, what moment this frozen moment from 1948, sent to her in this moment decades later, would entangle with in her life when the card arrived. What memories would it spark? What connections would it forge? In what directions would it prompt her imagination?

As the bus drove past my house I looked up at the attic skylight, unlit, no one there, and as we continued toward Dundee I felt I could almost see traces of yesterday's contrails left imprinted on the route as, in my imagination, I'd followed the same course I was actually taking today. And at lunchtime, since my office is only ten minutes' walk from where James McIntosh Patrick painted his view, and since that view was still very much in my mind, I made a point of going there again, walking past the gate, looking toward the Tay Bridge, its familiar bulk and shape dominating the outlook now as then.

* * *

I've tried to take the likeness of what I've called a moment. I hope the sentences I've crafted trace out enough of its isobars to give some sense of its prevailing winds and weather. But I'm well aware of how elusive a phenomenon it is and how difficult to trap in any word-cage. Unlike *The Tay Bridge from My Studio Window*, I've not added features that aren't there. To take an obvious example, the iron railings shown on the garden wall, which cast such a pleasing filigree of shadows on the ground, had been removed before 1948. Like iron railings all over the country, they'd been requisitioned for armaments during the war. They were painted from memory, not from what actually met McIntosh Patrick's eye as he looked out his studio window. And this makes me wonder what else alongside the actual may have been drawn from what he remembered or imagined. But maybe it's worth recalling to mind a comment of Arundhati Roy's that I think applies as much to painting as it does to writing: "Fiction and nonfiction are only different techniques of storytelling."

Things change. Even the most familiar scene isn't static, invariable. However much it may give the impression of permanence, nothing stays exactly as it appears at the moment we perceive it. Trees bud, leaves form and fall, walls are built, railings are fixed into them, then taken down again and smelted into armaments. Clouds go through their themes and variations. The seasons turn; time passes. The breeze comes and goes, marking the waters of the Tay with endless arrays of patterns.

The moment I've tried to measure out in words isn't something separate, independent, isolable, static—however tempting it may be to see it thus. To present it on its own, in isolation, with clear boundaries is artificial. It's linked, contiguous, adjacent, bound to the surge and flow of being. Like any moment, it's mobile, fluid, and connected to the huge expanse of time and space of which it's so minuscule a constituent part.

Real telepathy, if it existed, would have no need for any intermediary medium, whether words or paint. Mind could speak directly to mind; my thoughts could become your thoughts, yours become mine. We could savor another person's experience directly, without the crutch of symbols. In the absence of such a faculty, if we wish to share the cargo of our consciousness, we need to set up the red-clothed table with its cage and conjure into being whatever creatures we want to display from our menageries of experience.

I'm not a storyteller, let alone a master storyteller like Stephen King. The narratives that interest me are keyed less to the adrenaline of horror, more to the phenomenology of the everyday. The tempo of my sentences isn't geared to action and suspense. I hope my reflective tone and pace won't be condemned as the "prissy attention to detail that takes all the fun out of writing," which King understandably derides. Fast-paced fiction is enormously enjoyable. But for whatever reason, when it comes to writing, my inclinations dance to another tune. I'm more interested in the utterly extraordinary creatures that populate our everyday experience than in any invented rabbit, however intriguing we make the numerals painted on its back. I need no invention to create what's incredible. It lies all around us; it can become evident with no more stimulus than hearing a bus drive past.

An essay like this, far from setting some cracking pace to pull readers along from one thrill to the next is, rather, an attempt to slow things down, lasso a transient moment as it canters past and confine it for a while in the corral of language, there to look at it and be amazed. Once we stop to examine them closely, ordinary things are quite astonishing in what they consist of, what they contain, what they connect with. Astonishing, too, is the power of words to send thoughts and feelings, impressions and ideas, from one mind to another, even though those minds may be separated by gulfs of time and space and situation. Of course, "We cannot cage the minute / Within its nets of gold." But we can convey more than an inkling of the lustrous sheen that shines and sparkles all around us.

Benchmarks

It's summer—a fine, sunny day, warm enough to be comfortable in a short-sleeved linen shirt. Because I walked for miles yesterday on a path that winds its way enticingly along the coast, I'm tired. I went far further than I meant to, and a lack of energy today is the result. But it's too nice to stay indoors, so I decide to take a short stroll in the Botanic Garden that's close to where I live. I say a *stroll.* In fact I sit a lot. The garden is amply provided with wooden benches. These are placed at regular intervals along the main path and in various well-chosen niches amid the bushes, flowers, and trees. I have a pleasant afternoon, enjoying the diversity of plants in all their varied livery of size, shape, color, and fragrance. The rich bird and insect life that flourishes here is also a delight. Walking short distances and then sitting is well-geared to the exhaustion I feel from yesterday, and it's nice to pause at the different vantage points the benches offer and just watch the world go by, taking in the gentle waves of circumstance that happen in this place. It sounds like a tranquil way to pass the time, and yes, to some extent it is. But this garden idyll also brings me face to face with death.

* * *

Perhaps that's to overdramatize things. It's not as if I meet the Grim Reaper on his rounds; there's no hooded, scythe-carrying figure lurking in the undergrowth, waiting to ambush the unwary. The Botanic Garden is peaceful and well-ordered. There's no one obviously ill or grievously wounded here. We're far removed from any war zone; there's no stench of battlefield carrion or the sound of wailing survivors gathered at some mass grave that holds the victims of massacre. We're nowhere near the site of famine, earthquake, flood, or any other disaster, whether natural or of human agency. This is a lovely place, a little oasis of beauty that should banish such ugly images and be soothing to the spirit. I feel its therapeutic touch. It's just that each of the benches marks a death. They all carry memorial plaques. This bestows a funerary undertow to the garden's calm surface waters. My thoughts are pulled under, into the turbulence of considering mortality.

Some plaques only give a name, with dates of birth and death. Others include something about how the person loved this place. The names of those who mourn them are sometimes added. One inscription, typical of many, reads:

In loving memory of
Anne McMahon (1926–2003)
Who loved these gardens
Dougie and family

I know it's fanciful, I know the individuals named on these benches aren't somehow imbued in their timber. Nonetheless, I can't help feeling that I'm sitting with the dead. Each time I stop at a bench and read its inscription, it's almost as if a shadow of the person named takes form and sits, wraith-like, beside me. As I go around the garden, sitting in turn with Nicky, Edith, Bill, with Stella and John and Christine, with David, Mary, and Douglas, I find my thoughts turning more and more to our shared finitude. Encountered one after the other, these little brass plaques are like cognitive tuning forks all set to the same minor key. Their repeated soundings as I read them put my mind into a somber register. It's part elegiac, part alarmed, part resigned, part reflective, as I muse about these deaths that have happened, and mine that lies ahead.

* * *

Death.

Can anything usefully be said about it? Or is it simply an inevitable eventuality, an end that mirrors our beginning, each pointing to the vast swathes of time that don't contain us; the before and after that bookend with unnerving duration the brevity of our existence? Is it better to think about death, try to prepare for it, or just do our best to forget about it and get on with things until our own demise looms so closely we can't ignore it any longer?

In this peaceful place, on this sunny day, it would be easy to be lulled into thinking that life will go on just as it is, at this untroubled pace, to lose sight of its inevitable destination. The memorial plaques on the benches are reminders of the guillotine moment waiting to fall at some point, terminating the connection between now and next. The vital artery of being that carries us all forward, moment by moment, holds in its blueprint an unstoppable event. Wired into its water is cessation for each of us, without exception. Every life that's carried in time's flow will stop.

* * *

I'm aware that what I'm attempting may look ridiculous. It's easy to mock someone writing about death. And perhaps they deserve it. Isn't there something risible about the disparity in scale between writer and topic? It's a bit like a dog or cat attempting a treatise on cosmology. It's reminiscent, too, of those old belletrists who wrote dutifully serious essays on topics so wide-ranging ("On Love," "On Time," "On Beauty") that their few pages seem ludicrously feeble, a paltry scratching at surfaces beneath which lurk enormous depths. When it comes to death, such set pieces offer a clutch of sentences that, however eloquent, amount to very little. They tell us nothing we didn't know before we read them, give no answers to questions that concern us, only reiterate the obvious in flowery prose, and perhaps exhort us to do what we already know we should do—not squander the brief time allotted to us.

In my defense, I'm only trying to note down what I felt. I'm not interested in belles lettres. I don't want to preach a sermon or provide a philosophy. I'm not addressing some massive abstract whose scale makes any individual's attempt to grapple with it seem absurdly insignificant. What spurred these reflections is small-scale and specific: the inscriptions on some wooden benches. My aim is modest. I don't want to tackle any great universal theme, at least not directly. My approach is more tangential, personal, limited. I want only to put into order the swarm of ideas, distracting as insects, that jostled my contentment on an afternoon's stroll in the Botanic Garden. If, in so doing, a glint of larger perspectives gleams through my chosen point of focus, so be it, I can't prevent it. I'll be pleased if what I write functions at least in part as a lens, darkened with the protective of particularity, something that lets us look toward such bright light without being dazzled. But it's not my intention to stare directly at death's sun. I want simply to examine the unexpected turn an afternoon's stroll took.

* * *

In any case, two of the reasons the memorial plaques interest me have nothing to do with death. I like them, first, because they're such story-rich fragments. Each one is potently suggestive of whatever individual life they commemorate. One blogger who writes about the phenomenon of these kinds of memorials puts the matter nicely:

> Each bench tells a story of someone loved and remembered. These are not celebrities, they are you and me. . . . inscriptions always tell you something about the person and make me wonder about their story. (www.memorialbenchstories.wordpress.com/).

I too am made to wonder. Even when very little is said about them, the plaques always nudge my imagination into picturing something of the person named. It's almost as if what's given is a piece of a shattered mirror that still holds a tiny fraction of someone's reflection. It glitters with the promise of reconstruction, of discovering some semblance of the whole.

The second nonmorbid reason for the magnetism exerted by these little inscriptions, lies in the fact that they provide multiple examples of a fundamental challenge that, as a writer, I'm faced with every day: how to put what you want to say into words, clearly and economically. The brass plaques impose a stricter version of the discipline of the page. They demand expression within limited space. Whoever composes them has to say whatever they want to say about someone they held dear in the handful of words that will fit on this tiny surface area. Looking at the plaques makes me think of haiku, the Japanese poetic form that compresses expression into just seventeen syllables.

I know the plaques have no literary or philosophical agenda; their concision is a practical upshot of their scale. Nonetheless, they raise some interesting and difficult questions. How do we represent someone in just a few sentences or phrases? What is it that we most want to remember about them and how is this best put into words? Do we wish to convey more than name and dates of birth and death? And what exactly do these tell us? When we flense away the inessentials, what's left? How much can we condense a life? Under the radical constraints imposed by a haiku or a plaque, what is gained and what is lost? Is there a verbal minimum below which meaning has insufficient oxygen to take hold and flourish? At what point, if we incrementally increase what's said, do we cross a line so that what's crucial gets diluted with the merely secondary? Putting anything into words means changing it as well as communicating it. If we keep within the small compass afforded by a plaque, do we lessen or increase the chances of distortion? Does small scale impose the discipline of focus, help us to distill things to their essence, or does it cripple and disfigure with the amount that it excises?

* * *

Encountered singly, I doubt if any of the plaques on these memorial benches would have had much impact, beyond sparking speculation about life stories and concise expression. But the flotilla of inscriptions I met with that afternoon had a powerful cumulative effect. I've come to think of them as acting like a swarm of microbial particles, all carrying jigsaw pieces of the same complex ailment. Breathing in one or two would have been inconsequential. But en masse they infected me with a heightened sense of mortality.

Sitting with my arm resting along the back of one of the benches, I grasped the wood and squeezed, felt its rough grain hard against the cushioned tension of my hand. And looking at my bare arm stretched out on the wood, the muscles flexed, the veins prominent in the summer warmth, I felt with keener emphasis than usual the fact of my own fleetingness. It was as if the blunt edge of that background awareness of finitude that's always with us had been honed into scalpel sharpness. It cut to the quick with the realization that my hold on the world is similarly brief to my hand's grip on the wood. And it made me ask afresh that perennially puzzling question: am I anything more than a momentary assemblage of cells and nerve impulses, a muscled piece of sentience, transient in its manifestation, doomed soon not to exist?

The cloud of inscriptions jostled together in my mind like flints. Their sparks kindled a valedictory mood. It made me want to bid my hand goodbye, my wrist, my forearm, and my shoulder. Every part of my warm, cherished, familiar body. A time will come soon enough when there'll be nothing to will my hand to grip, nothing to feel the resistance of the wood, or savor the rough texture of its grain. Nothing will remain that could instruct the simple action of sitting down, or tightening muscles, let alone holding a pen and writing sentences. Soon there will be nothing to generate such impulses, nothing to obey them, nothing to sit or grip or write with. Name all your body parts, your unique corporeal signature of selfhood, and in anticipation bid them all farewell, in sure and certain knowledge that they'll vanish. That afternoon, I came to feel waterlogged with the realization that I'd become as rendered down and mute as the gravel on the ground and the sand from yesterday's walk still clinging to my boots. The massive fact of nonbeing envelops us; a seeming infinity of nullity surrounds the fragile ephemera of consciousness.

* * *

Sometimes the dates declare the tragedy of those who died too young. Derek Shedden, gone at twenty-one: "His laughter will always be missed." Kevin Pilkington, just four years older, who left Emma grieving and saying, "I'll love you forever," signing off her inconsolable loss with three x'd kisses. Such premature deaths, devastating to families, are witnessed to by several of the benches. But mostly, thankfully, the dates don't jar like this. Though of course bereavement hurts at whatever point it falls, at least with those who reach their eighties and nineties there's a sense they enjoyed a decent span of years.

I know they're intended to memorialize, to keep someone in mind, but when I read them the plaques on the benches seem more like a kind of rosary of anonymity, reducing whoever's named to extinction's common denominator. Perhaps the benches preserve the memory of particular individuals for those who knew them, but for me they're just a set of extracts from the endless roll call of the dead. Changing the names, or the dates of birth and death, would make little difference to the fundamental message each plaque shouts out: "This person's gone; they're mourned by partner, family, friends. This place was special to them." And each shout has an echo that reverberates beyond what's said. Whatever's written on the plaque, the subtext, glaring in its unsubtle inescapability, is that everyone will follow to oblivion those named in this fashion. The memorial plaques may swim against the current of forgetting for a while, but soon enough they'll falter. Time's irresistible flow buries everything—all of us—beneath it.

Often that afternoon, as I read the captions, imagined the unmet person taking ghostly form on the bench beside me, I didn't just speculate about the life they might have led, the kind of individual they were, and if we'd met, what sort of conversation we might have had. I also thought of them as they were over the full span of their existences, from the moment of conception to the moment that their breathing ceased. I passed in review their babyhood and infancy, their childhood, schooldays, working lives, their dreams, their fears, their loves and hates. And I tried to bring into focus the stupendous fact that, underlying this diversity of perished people, they all connect, sharing profound commonalities of origin, end, and experience. Whatever narrative variations we weave, we're part of one story, the human saga, written on Earth in the syllabary of individual lives. We are like letters in some vast alphabet that forms and reforms its patterns and sequences repeatedly. But beyond our commonsense constructions we're unsure what meaning, if any, is spelled out.

* * *

The bench plaques mostly just include the name and dates of the person commemorated. Occasionally, though, a little more is added. So on one bench, beneath the name—Douglas Sinclair—this assertion follows: "Nature's peace will flow through you as sunshine flows into trees." It's an appealing thought, that as you sit in this tranquil place, surrounded by a profusion of beautiful plants and lulled by birdsong, a kind of healing will occur by way of a benign, invisible osmosis; that the garden offers some natural balm, a curative that happens as naturally as photosynthesis. I know how therapeutic the natural world can be, how restoring to the spirit, yet what I experienced that afternoon was anything but peaceful. It felt more as if the plaques had subtly cut incisions in the flesh of my everyday assumptions, revealing, as shocking as glimpsing underlying bone, the glint of elemental things—transience, loss, extinction—rock hard beneath the commonplace.

Often now I think of the benches at night, when the Botanic Garden is closed and everyone has gone away. Is it the absences they mark that make me picture them in this lonely nocturnal setting, when the gates are locked and the garden is deserted? I'm not sure. No matter the time of day, the weather, or the season, no matter whether any people are there to see them, the benches with their plaques remain. Like books stuck open at one page, they announce the same message whether or not it's being read, invisibly pulsing out, like little beacons, whatever it is their few words have been crafted to relate.

How many years will they last for? Even if they're carefully maintained—varnished, painted, rot kept at bay—they'll one day crumble, the plaques eventually become illegible after long exposure to the elements. By then, everyone who remembered the individuals memorialized will themselves have passed away. No doubt some in turn will be named on benches not yet made. (Is the wood for them growing somewhere even as I write this sentence?) And perhaps someone like me sitting on them one day decades hence will find their thoughts nudged into thinking about finitude, become yet another person musing about death.

And all the while, as the benches sit there in sunlight and in moonlight, the processes of life go on all around them—another always open book, but one we only read fractions of. We notice the leaves and flowers, hear rain falling, feel sun upon our skins; we're sensitive to light and dark, to hot and cold, the turning of the seasons. But our customary perspectives aren't geared to the intricacies of what happens beneath what's immediately obvious. We focus on the simplifications we can detect with our unaided senses. Cut to a calibration that measures out its ambit of concern on a scale we can keep pace with, our outlook is blinkered, shielded from the true dimensions of time and space in which everything is cradled. The hum and buzz of material and metabolism, the balance of interactions that sculpt the landscape and the lives around us, what happens at a cellular and atomic level is set at an inaudible pitch unless we deliberately attune our imaginations to catch it.

* * *

The fine weather means the garden is busy. As I stroll and sit, my choice of where to stop is often determined simply by which benches are left unoccupied. In my mood of plaque-tuned reverie, the other sitters add emphasis and poignancy to the cluster of commemorated dead. An elderly, frail-looking lady sits reading on a bench positioned in the shade of a magnificent tulip tree. Will she live to see the leaves take on their autumn burnish? Will she witness another spring? What size was the tulip tree when the egg and sperm that made her first fused together? What size will it have reached a decade after she's no longer here to see it? When she stands up, puts her book in a canvas shoulder bag, and walks unsteadily away, she's like a marker buoy. Her steps trace out a boundary between two great oceans: the living and the dead, the present and the absent. Soon enough she'll vanish to the other side and her being here in the world become no more than a memory, soon to be forgotten. Each moment we occupy is underlain by those who came before us; history is swollen with its cargo of the dead.

When I walk past a bench I sat on earlier it's occupied by a hot and tired-looking pregnant woman. There's a toddler beside her asleep in a pushchair. The bench is inscribed,

In memory of my twin sister
Mary St George Fowlie 1935–2007.

However close the ties that bind us—the intimacy of having a twin, the love between parents and children, the passionate attachment of lovers, the sense of closeness that pregnancy engenders, the relationships forged with friends and within families—all the threads that weave our cocoons of belonging will be cut as we fall into the nothingness of nonexistence.

Sitting on a bench that's "In memory of Stella Barkla 1913–1997 [and] Hugh M Barkla 1913–2001," there's a young couple oblivious to everything except each other. They provide a symbol almost as unsubtle as lovers copulating on a grave. Here in this little cameo moment (a man and woman in their twenties sitting kissing on a bench that commemorates a man and a woman who died in their eighties) is a picture that acts like a little icon of the human condition.

* * *

Those commemorated in this way represent the tiniest of minorities. If all the dead were provided with such monuments, the world would soon become a tangle of benches dotted with constellations of plaques, a planet-wide wasteland of memorial seating with no room left for the living to get on with living. Most of us leave behind no durable marker of our time here. For those who do, it's usually no more than a headstone. But many have no grave; ashes are mostly scattered without indication of dates or identities. We may be held in others' memories for a while, but for all of us our presence here on Earth, whatever time and place we occupied, will soon be followed by an uncommemorated absence. Before long, our names won't hold any trace of us; they'll mean nothing to anyone living; we'll be utterly extinguished. This is just the way it is. We live. We die. As a mortal, sentient creature, I guess it's only natural now and then to ponder finitude, in the same way as if I were incarcerated in some underground cell, I'd search it meticulously, repeatedly, eager to find a possible escape route.

As I try to put my thoughts in order I'm again struck by a sense of futility, the absurdity of adding to all that's been written already on this theme. What could my voice add to the many voices that have already spoken about death? Through the ages scholars and saints and scientists, poets, priests, and philosophers have written about our end—wisely, foolishly, lyrically, clumsily, in puzzled anguish, and in pompous certainty. What can I add? And why bother anyway? Why talk about the unpalatable obvious? With such uncomfortable things, perhaps it's best not to taste them till we have to. Why not just avoid them, choose something more cheerful to write about?

The little plaques on the Botanic Garden memorial benches made my thoughts unexpectedly somber on a lovely summer afternoon and left me feeling the need for comfort. I'm not sure there's any to be found, but as I sought it some words of Montaigne's came back to mind. They're from his essay "That to philosophize is to learn to die." Montaigne is alert to the symmetry of our nonexistence, the fact that what happens after death mirrors what happens before birth. He puts it like this:

> As our birth brought us the birth of all things, so will our death bring us the death of all things. Wherefore it is as foolish to lament that we shall not be alive a hundred years from now as it is to lament that we were not alive a hundred years ago.

If I were to have a memorial bench, these are the words I'd like inscribed on it. I'm not sure why, but simply stating the facts of the matter clearly, facing up to our transience, looking at our situation without blinking, without reaching for some spurious comfort is,—for all its bleakness—strangely exhilarating. But perhaps this is just an illusion of the moment. Maybe as death comes closer I'll crave the kind of fantasy that dusts over uncomfortable truths with the sugar of happy-ever-after endings. Whatever benchmark I might be given (in the unlikely event of being remembered), it won't concern me. By the time it's inscribed I'll have slipped the leash of words, succumbed to what Philip Larkin calls "the anaesthetic from which none come round."

NOTES

Few essayists wish to embrace footnotes. Too often these smack of what anthropologist Daniel Miller calls "pretentious obfuscation." This results in "vast circulations of obscure citation" serving little purpose beyond demonstrating that the author has been "tempted by the promise of an easy claim to cleverness." *What Is It Like to Be Alive?* quite deliberately contains no footnotes. However, on a few occasions it seemed apt to identify the sources I draw on. [Daniel Miller's comments are taken from his *Stuff* (Cambridge, U.K.: Polity Press, 2010), 79.]

INTRODUCTION

For "the infinite suggestiveness of common things," see Alexander Smith, *Dreamthorp: Essays Written in the Country* (London: Strahan, 1863), 25. For "At heart, the essay is the voice of the individual," see Graham Good's preface to *The Encyclopedia of the Essay*, ed. Tracy Chevalier (London: Fitzroy Dearborn, 1997), xxi.

Mary Oliver's poem "Bones" is in *Why I Wake Early: New Poems* (Boston: Beacon, 2004), 4.

For "Language is the soul's ozone layer and we thin it at our peril," see Sven Birkerts, *The Gutenberg Elegies: The Fate of Reading in an Electronic Age* (London: Faber & Faber, 1994), 133.

SPLINTER

Bruce Bernhard, *Humanity and Inhumanity: The Photographic Journey of George Rodger* (London: Phaidon, 1994), 97.

Primo Levi, *If This Is a Man* and *The Truce*, trans. Stuart Woolf (London: Penguin, 1979), 390–91.

Judith Miller, *One, By One, By One: Facing the Holocaust* (New York: Simon & Schuster, 1990), 287.

Susan D. Moeller, *Compassion Fatigue* (London: Routledge, 1999), 47.

Susan Sontag, *On Photography* (London: Penguin, 1979), 19, 20, 24.

IMAGES OF HALLOW HILL

The most detailed account of the archaeology of Hallow Hill, to which I am indebted, remains Edwina Proudfoot et al., "Excavations at the Long Cist Cemetery on the Hallow Hill, St Andrews, Fife, 1975-77," *Proceedings of the Society of Antiquaries of Scotland 126* (1996): 387–454.

LEARNING TO SEE GOLDCRESTS

The epigraph is from that classic of nature writing, J. A. Baker's *The Peregrine* (1967). See *The Complete Works of J. A. Baker*, ed. John Fanshawe (London: Collins, 2010), 23.

Joy Williams's "Save the Whales, Screw the Shrimps" first appeared in *Esquire*. It is reprinted in Justin Kaplan (ed), *The Best American Essays 1990* (New York: Ticknor & Fields, 1990), 262–75.

Jean-Henri Fabre's story of stealing a stonechat's egg can be found in *Fabre's Book of Insects* (New York: Dover, 1998), 2. This is a handy compendium that selects material out of the extensive writings of this great naturalist. His *Souvenirs entomologiques*, published in ten volumes between 1879 and 1907, are a model of the close observation of nature. His interests are by no means confined to insects. For Darwin's comments on Fabre, see Susan Grant's "Reflections: Fabre and Darwin: A Study in Contrasts," *BioScience* 26, no. 6 (1976): 395–98.

Brian Vesey-Fitzgerald's suggestion of an envelope and half a sheet of notepaper as a weight comparison for goldcrests is given in his *A Third Book of British Birds and Their Nests* (Loughborough: Wills & Hepworth, 1956), n.p.

John Muir's famous comment about the interconnectedness of things can be found in *My First Summer in the Sierra* (Boston: Houghton Mifflin, 1911), 211.

Specifically on goldcrests, the following material was useful:

- Svein Haftorn, "Egg-Laying and Regulation of Egg Temperature during Incubation in the Goldcrest *(Regulus regulus),*" *Ornis Scandinavica (Scandinavian Journal of Ornithology),* 9, no.1 (1978): 2–21.
- Svein Haftorn, "Energetics of Incubation by the Goldcrest in Relation to Ambient Air Temperature and the Geographical Distribution of the Species *(Regulus regulus),*" *Ornis Scandinavica (Scandinavian Journal of Ornithology),* 9, no.1 (1978): 22–30.
- International Union for Conservation of Nature (IUCN), "BirdLife International. 2018. *Regulus regulus. The IUCN Red List of Threatened Species 2018.*" www.iucnredlist.org/species/22734997/132183740.
- L. Jasso, "Autumn Migration of the Goldcrest (*Regulus regulus*) in the Western Krkonoše Mountains in 2001–2008," *Sylvia* 48 (2012): 126–33.
- Jochen Martens and Martin Päckert, "Family Regulidae (Kinglets & Firecrests)," in *Handbook of*

the Birds of the World, ed. Josep Del Hoyo et al., vol. 11 (Barcelona: Lynx Edicions, 2006), 330–49.

- Martin Päckert et al., "Radiation of Goldcrests *Regulus regulus:* Evidence of a New Taxon from the Canary Islands," *Journal of Avian Biology* 37, no. 4 (2006): 364–80.
- Randi Eidsmo Reinertsen, Svein Haftorn, and Ellen Thaler, "Is Hypothermia Necessary for the Winter Survival of the Goldcrest (*Regulus regulus)?" Journal of Ornithology* 129, no. 4 (1988): 433–37.
- Ellen Thaler, *Die Goldhähnchen* (Madgeburg: Die Neue Brehm Bücheri, 1990). For a summary in English of key points, see Tim Birkhead, *The Most Perfect Thing: Inside (and Outside) a Bird's Egg* (London: Bloomsbury, 2016), 189–90.

For more general ornithological background:

- Ruth Bellairs and Mark Ormond, *The Atlas of Chick Development*, 3rd ed. (Oxford: Academic Press, 2014).
- *Birds of Conservation Concern 5, British Birds*, 114, no. 12 (December 2021): 732–47.
- Tim Birkhead, *The Most Perfect Thing: Inside (and Outside) a Bird's Egg* (London: Bloomsbury, 2016).
- Charles Deeming and Mark Ferguson, eds., *Egg Incubation* (Cambridge: University of Cambridge Press, 1995).
- Garrett Dyke and Gary Kaiser, eds., *Living Dinosaurs: The Evolutionary History of Modern Birds* (Oxford: Wiley

Blackwell, 2011).

- Frank B. Gill, *Ornithology*, 2nd ed. (New York: W. H. Freeman, 1995).
- Noble S. Proctor and Patrick Lynch, *Manual of Ornithology* (New Haven, Conn.: Yale University Press, 1993).
- Alexis L. Romanoff and Anastasia J. Romanoff, *The Avian Egg* (New York: Wiley, 1949).

As useful touchstones for thinking about matters of size and perspective, I relied on J. S. Haldane's "On Being the Right Size," in his *Possible Worlds* (London: Chatto & Windus, 1927), 18–26; and Thomas Nagel's "What Is It Like to Be a Bat?" in *The Philosophical Review* 83, no. 4 (1974): 435–50.

ACKNOWLEDGMENTS

Parts of this book were written while I was a Royal Literary Fund (RLF) Fellow at the University of Dundee. Not only has the RLF Fellowship provided the kind of financial security writers rarely enjoy, but the way in which the scheme is operated does much to bolster a writer's sense of literary self-worth. Under the deft but light-touch leadership of Steve Cook and David Swinburne, the Fellowship offers a wonderfully supportive milieu in which to work. Steve and David have, I suspect, played a significant role in moving many books toward publication. I'm grateful for the part they've played in doing so with this one.

"Images of Hallow Hill" could not have been written without input from Edwina Proudfoot, who was responsible for the 1975–77 excavation of that site. I'm grateful to her for giving up so much of her time to talk to me about what was discovered. Thanks also to Jane Freel and staff at Fife Cultural Trust for allowing me to examine artifacts recovered from cist 54.

Versions of several of the essays here have been published singly. Thank you to *The Adirondack Review*, *Cutleaf*, *Delmarva Review*, *Irish Pages*, *Northwords Now*, *Queen's Quarterly*, *Taint Taint Taint Literary Magazine*, and *Terrain.org*. I'm grateful to the editors of these journals, not only for allowing me to reprint the essays here but also for providing valuable encouragement along the way.

Thank you to Robert Atwan and Phillip Lopate, key figures in the resurgence of the contemporary essay, whose work has done so much to alert people to the existence and potential of this still-too-often-marginalized literary genre. It has meant a lot to have their generous endorsements of my work.

This is my second book with EastOver Press. (*Hidden Cargoes* appeared in 2022.) In an early communication I was told: "We are all writers ourselves. Our goal is to treat you as we want to be treated." It has been a pleasure to work with a publisher that puts this ethos into practice so unfailingly. Thank you to Walter Robinson, Kelly March, and Louisa Castner for all the time, energy, and talent that they've devoted to moving *What Is It Like to Be Alive?* from raw typescript to published book.

Some writers claim not to look at or be influenced by reviews of their work. I am not one of them. Comment from reviewers, and from ordinary readers, provides an important stimulus for thinking about what I'm doing. I find it helpful to stand back from my writing every now and then and look at it through other people's perspectives. The feedback I received on earlier books provided valuable touchstones on the long, hard route that led from initial ideas to the publication of this one. I'm grateful to the following reviewers: Patricia Craig, Walter Cummins, Frances Devlin-Glass, Kirsty Gunn, Glenn Hooper, Marion Naugrette-Fournier, David Robinson, Denis Sampson, Eoghan Smith, Rob Volmarr, and Ellen Wiles. Unpublished but no less perceptive comments have been offered by Mark Charlton, Mary Hood, Graham Johnston, Maren O. Mitchell, Maeve Nolan, Dorcas Sohn, and Andy Wainwright.

Writing claims time in abundance, our most precious and least renewable natural resource. I'm grateful to Jane, Lucy, and Laura for their good-humored forbearance when it comes to the temporal demands my books make on family life.

ABOUT THE AUTHOR

Chris Arthur was born in Belfast and grew up in Northern Ireland during the Troubles. Following a period working as warden on a nature reserve on the shores of Lough Neagh, the largest lake in the British Isles and Northern Ireland's enigmatic geographical heart, he went to university in Scotland. After completing his MA and PhD, he spent some time as a TV researcher and then as a schoolteacher, before taking up academic posts at the Universities of Edinburgh and St Andrews. On being appointed to a lectureship at what was then St David's University College (later the University of Wales, Lampeter), he moved to Welsh-speaking rural Ceredigion and lived there for over a decade. When Lampeter merged with a neighbouring college and began to embrace priorities and policies with which he disagreed, he resigned and returned to Scotland to concentrate full-time on his writing. In 2014 he became a Fellow with the Royal Literary Fund.

He's author of eight previous essay collections, most recently *Hidden Cargoes* (2022) and *Hummingbirds Between the Pages* (2018). A new and selected essays volume, *Words of the Grey Wind*, was published in 2009.

In addition to his books, Chris has published in a wide range of journals. His work has also appeared in *The Best American Essays* and is often included in that series' 'Notable Essays' lists. According to *Publishers Weekly*, "Arthur is proof that the art of the essay is flourishing." Robert Atwan has described him as "among the very best essayists in the English language today." Phillip Lopate reckons that he's "one of our greatest living essayists."

Chris's writing prizes include: a Theodore Christian Hoepfner Award, the Monroe K. Spears Essay Prize, the Akegarasu Haya International Essay Prize, *Times Higher*/Palgrave Macmillan Writing Prize in the Humanities, and the Gandhi Foundation's Aitchtey Memorial Essay Prize.

Further information can be found at www.chrisarthur.org.

www.ingramcontent.com/pod-product-compliance
Lightning Source LLC
Chambersburg PA
CBHW060905210726
48293CB00006B/1967